Straight Advice: How to Market Art Online

PROFITABLE ADVICE AND USEFUL IDEAS FOR
ARTISTS ON WEBSITES, EMAIL MARKETING,
BLOGGING AND MORE

I0392437

Barney Davey

Bold Star Communications
SCOTTSDALE, AZ

Barney Davey/Art Marketing News / Bold Star Communications
PO Box 25386
Scottsdale, AZ 85255
ArtMarketingNews.com

Book Layout ©2013 BookDesignTemplates.com

Ordering Information:
Quantity sales. Special discounts are available on quantity purchases by corporations, associations, and others. For details, contact the "Special Sales Department" at the address above.

Straight Advice: How to Market Art Online Now/ Barney Davey. — 1st ed.
ISBN-13: 978-1535391344
ISBN-10: 1535391340

Contents

For My Visual Artist and Fine Art Photographer Friends

In marketing I've seen only one strategy that can't miss – and that is to market to your best customers first, your best prospects second and the rest of the world last. – John Romero

CHAPTER 1

Marketing Art Online

A wise man will make more opportunities than he finds. – Francis Bacon, Irish painter

Artists alive in this generation are the first ever to have tools that allow them to connect with buyers and sell to them directly. The internet has changed our buying habits. We can now get so close and learn so much about anything we want to buy, and then e-commerce, UPS and FedEx make everything readily available. In many metro areas, consumers can order from Amazon and other retailers and get same-day deliveries. The marketing – and therefore the art world – is literally at our fingertips.

And we're not just talking commodity items. All sorts of high-end luxury products are sold online. Costco.com, for example, is now one of the world's largest diamond retailers. What all this means is that artists are free to find their own buyers and eliminate all the third-party gatekeepers that controlled the sale of art. It's a Brave New World.

Change doesn't come easy. It never has and never will. It took many people a long, long time to give up the horse and buggy, but eventually they came around. I'm betting some wondered what the heck took them so long once they saw the benefits of a motorcar.

The whole world, it seems, is online. The internet has changed everything. It certainly killed the trade magazine industry, including *Decor* magazine, which devastated me.

Before its demise, the 135-year-old publication was considered the "Bible" of the art business world. Its companion DECOR Expo trade shows had grown to massive events taking over half the enormous Georgia World Trade Center. Neither the magazine nor the shows could survive the withering waves of media and marketing changes that steamrolled industry after industry.

To say the internet is a disruptive force is an understatement. And here we all are, loving our cool technology. I love the good things that have come about and realize nothing stays the same. Either go with the tide and roll with it, or get pulled under and suffer the consequences.

Besides the internet giving me the ability to write books, create online courses and do free and paid online webinars that are then archived for future viewing on YouTube, what I love most about it is the freedom and career control it offers artists who embrace its possibilities.

No matter where you are on the ramp-up to using technology to market your art, you need to have enough information to help you make smart, informed decisions about how to use that technology and make it work for you. I wrote this book to give artists tips on using technology more efficiently.

This book is by no means encyclopedic. That would take a huge volume. One I'd be afraid to write because I know that, by the time I finished the last sentence, much of what I'd written would already be outdated. Besides, I don't think most artists want to be bogged down by too much information of any kind, especially technology.

Book Content Disclosure

The content of this book comes from a variety of sources. All of it is written by me, Barney Davey, the author. Some of it comes from previous books I have written. Some of it comes from blog posts I have written. A good deal of it is original content created for this book.

All of the previously published material has been carefully and thoroughly revised and re-edited to reflect the current state of marketing art. The challenge in writing anything about technology, it is a challenge, as mentioned above, to create content that is relevant, up-to-date, and accurate. I've done my best to do those things for you.

So enjoy this book with my best wishes for success in taming technology to your advantage for your art career.

CHAPTER 2

Understanding the Value of a Customer Persona

There is extraordinary chemistry that exists in long-term relationships. – Conrad Levinson

What Is a Customer Avatar?

A customer persona is also known as an avatar. Avatar is a fitting buzzword for a customer profile in our digital age.

A customer avatar is as close to a real person as you can imagine. It's an ideal composite of demographics, psychographics, characteristics, habits and behaviors of many people.

This content is borrowed from my How to Find Collectors training course. It's Lesson One in the training for a good reason. That's because, if you start trying to market your work without any idea of who'll buy it, you'll fail. Artists do not have the budget to do mass marketing and so it makes no sense to try.

Your art is specific to certain people. That's a good thing. Your first job as a marketer is to find the best prospective buyers of your work and then connect with them, and then to let them know that your art is available. It's up to them to decide if they're interested buyers. Remember, even if they aren't potential collectors now, they can still be active sources of referrals. And, their buying habits and needs may change over time.

Why You Need a Customer Avatar

Six things happen when you have an accurate avatar working for you:

1. Your prospects for new sales are prequalified.
2. Your cost per lead for new prospects gets much cheaper.
3. Prequalified prospects are much easier to convince and convert into buyers and collectors.
4. Leads that fit your avatar's description will make you the most money.
5. As buyers, they'll be your happiest customers, and they'll cause you the least problems.
6. Since few artists know to create an avatar, you give yourself a tremendous competitive advantage.

The more you can describe your customer in great detail, the better you can target where to look for prospects. The point is to spend less time and money going after fewer people to get more sales.

The Trout Fishing Analogy

If you are fishing for trout, you don't use shark bait.

If you're serious about trout fishing, you get the right equipment that will give you the best chance to catch trout. You also research to find the best spots to go trout fishing, and you study to learn the best techniques for fly casting.

Trout will never come to you. You have to go to them. To get good at trout fishing, you need practice. You need to study what trout like. You have to learn where you can find trout populations. Through study and practice, you begin to understand what trout like and how they act. Do they like fast-running water or slower streams? Are they hungrier at certain times of day? Do they swim close to the top of the water on sunny days?

There are hundreds, if not thousands, of nuances and things you can learn about trout and trout fishing that will make you more successful at catching them. The best fishermen put in many, many hours studying to become proficient. They make it their mission. They teach themselves to think and act like trout.

Without knowing who your best potential buyers and collectors are, you're wasting time casting about here and there with understandably inconsistent results. You have a limit to both the time and money you can spend finding customers. And so, to get the highest return on your investment, you need to learn as much as you can about your potential buyers. If you get as interested in learning about them as trout fishermen do about trout, you're going to succeed.

Direct-Buying Customers Are Your Key to a Profitable Future

Your most lucrative and best path to long-term success is selling directly to buyers and collectors. The only way to accomplish that is by knowing how to selectively target your top prospects. A refined customer avatar steers you to honing in on your highest value potential buyers. With it, you avoid wasting precious time and money.

Collectors vs. Buyers

All collectors are buyers. Not all buyers are collectors. Buyers are customers who make a purchase to fill a need, which is, most often a matter of interior design and decoration. Collectors buy art because they love art and artists. It thrills them to seek out new artists. They're into the whole scene. They take vacations to "art destinations" like Scottsdale, Santa Fe, Manhattan and so on. They want to support artists, too. Most importantly, they buy multiple pieces. It's a different mindset from a buyer with a single need.

They don't have to be art tourists to be art collectors. They only need to exhibit a passion for art and artists – and have enough disposable income to buy art.

This is an enormous distinction you cannot afford to overlook – your prospects have to have money to spend.

Unless you're most fortunate, you need both buyers and collectors. The latter are harder to find and take more time to develop. For that reason, your marketing should include methods of attracting both buyers and collectors. A right mix will give you a prosperous career.

Buyers Make Great Collectors

Everyone starts somewhere. All but a few collectors started out as buyers first. They might have started buying a limited edition print in a Thomas Kinkade gallery and found the whole process intriguing and fun. Armed with their new enthusiasm for buying art, they look now to upgrade their experience and buy originals or higher quality art.

In your career, you'll encounter many first-time buyers. Meeting them gives you a fantastic opportunity. You can help those who are inclined to become art collectors. Provide them with an appreciation of the value and enjoyment of collecting art and supporting artists. Not all buyers will become collectors, but if you make it your job to nurture your following you make it more likely for such an evolution to take place.

The Importance of Pinpointing Your Avatar

I realize many of you don't have scores of direct buyers. Don't feel alone. And don't feel bad if you have none. This is the case for many artists, especially early in your career.

I'm acutely aware that a lack of personal relationships with customers makes this exercise of defining your customer avatar harder. Nevertheless, you can't use a scarcity of information as an excuse for not doing this exercise. Whatever you come up with for now isn't set in stone. I suggest you go to your calendar right now and make a repeating quarterly date with yourself to review and update your customer avatar. It will evolve over time.

The worst-case scenario is that your first avatar will be all wrong. That's still better than taking the clueless route – the kind that involves throwing money at marketing with no idea of whether or not it will work. Being all wrong – and I doubt this will happen – still gives you a baseline. It allows you to exclude things, which is just as important as knowing what to add to the mix. It's a significant, advantageous money- and a time-saver to know who NOT to market to.

By describing your target market, you are segmenting who you most want as buyers and who are most likely to become collectors who buy from you many times.

Your description must be precise and focused. Too often, marketers stay too broad and general. This isn't helpful, and it's a waste of your time.

The more you pinpoint your ideal customers, the more you can use all your communications to make them feel comfortable with you in person and online. When you get this down, it's as if you've almost read their minds and walked in their shoes. You want to accurately identify their pain points, fears, frustrations, desires and dreams.

Think about what are pain points your prospective customers have regarding owning art. What concerns or questions do they have about owning art? When you have a feel for what goes on in their mind, it becomes easier for you to make a decision and feel good about helping buy your art. Use this information in the context of buying art. Pain points are most helpful when trying to solve a problem. To that extent, everyone with a blank wall or space has a problem. Everyone with inferior art that does not enhance a space has a problem. Everyone who owns art that no longer or never speaks to them has a problem. Anyone who's curious about owning original art but is hesitant because they are intimidated by the process also fits this description. Use your own experience to dig for your customer's needs.

New buyers can be afraid of making a mistake when buying art. How do they know if what they're buying is worth it? They might be frustrated that they haven't been able to find the art that suits their needs, that fills the space and makes them feel something. Sometimes they're looking for art that connects them to something, and they don't have a clue to that "something" or how to find it.

Besides having a clear idea of who your avatar is, you'll also know from these questions where to look for buyers and collectors and how to communicate with them. Edgy hip-hop art buyers will have a different vocabulary from purchasers of pet portraits or fine art photography.

What Information Goes into Creating an Avatar?

Start with what you know about those who've already bought your art. Are there some who've purchased multiple pieces? Don't be discouraged if you don't have this information yet. What I'm recommending is a process, not a test. You have to start somewhere and this is it.

Think about your art. Are there defining qualities to it? Are you working a niche? It's okay if you feel like this kind of introspection is challenging. It is! It's okay if your art doesn't fit comfortably into a "niche." Don't let this stop you. It's a hard process for everyone, harder for some. That's the ways things are in life – and in selling art. Regardless, the payoff will be even greater than any difficulty you faced in creating your avatar. Read on and learn the many ways to do that.

A useful avatar covers both the demographics and psychographics of your target audience. Clues are all around you. You just need to start tuning into the available information.

Here are some suggestions to will help you (think of yourself as an art avatar CSI):

- Look at your Facebook page to see who's liked it. Then look to see what else they like, and keep going down the rabbit hole.
- Check out your competition and who likes their pages. If you have other social media accounts, do the same thing. If your competition has a Twitter

account, then start looking to see who's following them. Look for trends.

- Go to the pages of your followers and your competitions' fans, read the bios, and look at their websites.

Visit successful galleries, artists' open studios and art fairs. Be observant about who's interested in your work, or work that's similar to yours. What are the reader demographics of magazines that might do a feature story on you or artists like you? Where do they reside? Are they city or rural dwellers? What is their education level? Do they fit into a definable ethnic, cultural, gender, age or professional group? What kind of home furnishings do they purchase? What kind of cars do they drive? What are their passions? Do they like travel, wine, beer, sports, cultural events or food fairs? Where do they take vacations? What kind of hobbies do they have? What charities, religious and political groups do they belong to? Are they members of associations? Are there Meetup.org groups where they're active?

Read reviews of books, art and related products on Amazon and elsewhere to look for clues about who's taking the time to write a review. Read comments on your blog, or blogs of competitors, or art magazines, or online sites that are simpatico with your work. Who's making those comments? What are their demographics?

There is a near-infinite amount of information if you're willing to do the research. But don't let that stop you either. There is quality information out there for you. You just have to be resourceful and determined. This is your business after all, and this exercise will pay dividends for decades to come.

Benefits of a Customer Avatar

By focusing your efforts on getting your best customers, you not only spend less money marketing to them, but you are also much more likely to enjoy buyers who will do the following: Spend more time and money with you. Give you repeat business. Are less inclined to haggle with you over prices. Represent the largest portion of your income. Give you honest feedback on your work. Refer your art to their family and friends. Generate priceless word-of-mouth buzz about you and your work. Make introductions to powerful connections such as gallery owners, designers, docents, media contacts and others.

When you know more about your potential buyers, it becomes easier to talk and communicate with them in their own language. It simplifies your marketing message. You can unify everything you're doing to appeal to your ideal customer. Your website, blog, email marketing and all other communications and branding can be written and created with your avatar in mind.

It's much easier to address a customer's desires, needs, frustrations and fears when you're confident that you know who that person is. It will help you with your pricing, too. And, it makes it easier to avoid marketing and communicating with those with whom you do not wish to associate.

Now your advertising will hit home instead of being generic and forgettable. You can tailor your messages to speak to your desired audience and tune out the rest. A dialed-in, tuned-in message is always going to have a greater effect than one trying to reach a mass audience. You can also anticipate and answer your buyers' objections before they're even asked. Choosing the most effective marketing media that your target customers are most likely to see becomes a snap.

The bottom line is that a tightly drawn avatar will boost your conversion rate, help you attract your best prospects and prevent you from losing money on ineffective marketing and advertising.

Personalize your avatar. When you're finished, give your avatar a name. Take it a step further and find an image that best represents the person you've described. Place that image someplace visible in your workspace to give you a steady visual reminder of who's right for you and why. You can start thinking about that buyer in creating your art, almost as if you're working on a commission.

Once you've answered all the suggested questions, and any custom questions you've added, you can turn it all into a story about your avatar. Here's an example:

Marjorie is a 48-year-old mother and soon-to-be grandmother. She's been married for 26 years to Hal, who runs a chain of dry cleaner stores. He's a second-generation owner of the business and has doubled it in size since he took it over 10 years ago. Marjorie works part-time in the business, *helping Hal oversee the backend by looking after the accounting and marketing parts of the operation. She also volunteers a few hours each week at the local hospital. Their combined annual owner take-home pay averages $175,000, making them HENRYs (High-Earner Not Rich Yet).*

They have three children. The oldest daughter has been married a year and is pregnant with their first grandchild. The younger two have finished college and have entered the workforce, leaving Marjorie and Mark empty nesters. This allows them more time to do the things they love. Hal's an avid golfer; Marjorie, a recreational player. They both like to travel, enjoy finding new places to eat and love finding new, affordable fine wines to drink. They enjoy cultural events from local theater to symphony concerts, and the occasional classic rock concert. They look forward to annual events in their area, such as the Great American Picnic put on by the Culinary Festival, which benefits the local fine art museum.

Marjorie has always been interested in fine art and took many classes in it in both high school and college. Hal has found through Marjorie's interest that he too takes a liking to fine art. Hal likes smoking cigars and has recently taken an interest in vintage automobiles. They attend a few local auto shows annually and have plans to go to Scottsdale some year during the annual Barrett-Jackson auto auction in January. That trip will allow them time to golf, enjoy fine dining, tour the local annual white tent art shows and the renowned Main Street area of Scottsdale with its many world-class galleries. When time allows, Marjorie wants to take some classes at the Scottsdale Art School.

While they have a comfortable, safe retirement and are enjoying the fruits of their labor from their small business, they're both concerned about being able to sell when they are ready to retire. This hits home more since none of their children have shown any desire to step into the family business. They've bought a few small pieces of original art and are considering the idea of buying more. However, they have some fears about overspending or buying the wrong kind of art. They want to be smart about what they do with their expenditures on art and other things. They like the idea of passing the art they buy along to their children and grandchildren. In many ways, they're ripe candidates for collecting art and supporting the work of artists whose work they love.

Although they're not afraid to spend money on vacations, art and potentially a collector car, they're still conservative and don't consider purchases they can't make with their disposable income. In other words, they don't borrow money to pay for their interests and passions.

I could continue on here, but you don't need a novella to get the idea. Your avatar's story can be as long as it needs to be. There's nothing wrong with writing as complete a background story as you can to help you formulate a fully fleshed out avatar. You're making your art for this person, and you'll do your customer hunting research and development based on those traits you explore and add to your avatar.

What about Multiple Avatars?

Multiple avatars are fine. In fact, most artists will have more than one ideal buyer or collector. You may have an avatar for a buyer that is much different from your collector avatar. This's normal and okay. You will, however, create problems for yourself if you have too many avatars. Remember, this is about specifics. If you're too spread out with your avatars, you'll make it too difficult to define your audience and fine-tune your marketing and focusing your efforts toward any particular group. And that was the point of a more targeted audience – and an avatar – to begin with.

So, if you find yourself with more than a few avatars, you may need to consider that your art creation may not be as focused as it needs to be. If may also be that you've saturated one of your target markets. It's better to put your efforts and budget into going deeper into your highest potential target markets than spreading yourself thin in too many areas. If you water down your marketing efforts by trying to attract too many various customers, you'll diminish their effectiveness and lose sales as a result. It will also affect your branding and online identity.

CHAPTER 3

Websites for Artists

In an endless jungle of websites with text-based content, a beautiful image with a lot of space and colour can be like walking into a clearing. It's a relief. – David McCandless

To begin with, every artist needs a website. Period. It's not optional. The debate is over. Artists and other small business people should no longer be debating whether having a website is necessary. Today, according to the Pew Research Center, when 85% of the U.S. population has internet access, it isn't an option. You need to be onboard and represented online.

One of the chief purposes of having a website is to help you sell and promote your art using the tremendous efficiencies of email marketing. Email is the most cost-effective method of getting your message out to a targeted list of buyers and collectors.

While the irritations with spam and social media have both reduced its effectiveness, email marketing is an essential part of your marketing mix. Collecting email addresses is a top-priority task for your business. Include an opt-in form or option as part all marketing efforts.

The internet has caused all manner of artists to reconsider how they get the products of their creation to market. I've often mentioned how the late artist Prince signaled a change. To some, it seemed a defiant act of career suicide when he abandoned traditional distribution channels – recording labels and music retailers – in favor of selling directly to his faithful fans through his website.

A few years later found him giving away millions of copies of his CD in advance of a series of concerts in London. He knew he would gain enough fans and sell enough tickets to more than cover that cost. He understood that the value of the publicity generated by that giveaway was worth millions.

Giving It Away and Getting It Back

The marketing tactics used by Prince and other artists who embraced the internet to reach their fans are worth noting. The Grateful Dead is the most downloaded and traded musical act in history. They proved a multimillion-dollar enterprise could be grown on the strength of giving away their product for free by allowing the copying and distribution of their live performances. In fact, they even provided a special place where those who taped their concerts could hook up their equipment.

In the process, the Grateful Dead created legions of dedicated fans, many of whom spent money on tickets, authorized recordings, and other ancillary and licensed products, the sales of which more than make up for the "loss" they suffered from the free distribution of otherwise marketable recorded music. Disruptive marketing tactics like these have helped to create what has become an ongoing and tectonic change in the allocation of information and entertainment, as well as literary and visual art.

The British band Radiohead put a new spin on such ideas when it released a downloadable CD and allowed its fans to pay whatever they thought it was worth, including nothing at all if they wished. And then, after more than a few million downloads and a lingering floodtide of resulting publicity, the band finally set minimum prices for the CD.

Both the Australian artist Hazel Dooney and British graffiti artist Banksy offer their fans high-quality digital downloads of their work. In Dooney's case, if you send your printed copy to her with a self-addressed and stamped return envelope, she will sign and return it to you. Both artists have generated positive, newsworthy acknowledgments of their generosity and in the process have created new fans and new levels of fan loyalty.

The internet has also combined with print-on-demand (POD) technology to provide a powerful technological tool allowing visual artists, writers and musicians to sell their creations directly to the public. The dynamics of these developments have affected how all parties involved, including consumers, retailers, distributors and publishers, receive and are compensated for goods delivered.

These days, in fact, consumers are doing their best to avoid once traditional means of distribution. They listen to music on the internet and over satellite broadcasts. They buy music downloads at Starbucks or from home or the office (which might be home) to play on their iPads or phones. To avoid annoying each other with phone calls and emails, they relentlessly type abbreviated text messages on their cell phones to be read at the receiver's convenience. They avoid commercials, too, by fast-forwarding prerecorded audio and visual programs, including DVRs that can be programmed to skip the interruptions (a.k.a. the commercials), all time-shifting strategies that give them greater control of product distribution and convenience.

The publishing industry has witnessed an explosion of self-published books. Just a few years ago, the idea of my writing and successfully self-publishing a book seemed out of the question. Now, formerly frustrated artists are using new publishing tools to take control of the ways their products reach their collectors, readers and listeners. It's not a time to be complacent about how you get your work to market.

What you need at the very least is an awareness of how distribution channels are evolving so you can judge the opportunities and pitfalls of the options now available to you. The inestimable American humorist, Will Rogers, couldn't have said it better: "Even if you're on the right track, you'll get run over if you just sit there."

The Internet Changed the Gallery Business Forever

While getting a sale on a first visit was always a tremendous challenge for a brick and mortar gallery, the internet has made it more difficult. It allows collectors to price shop and perform due diligence on the gallery's claim about the artist's reputation, the art's provenance and more. As a result, many galleries are carrying fewer prints because they recognize that originals don't have the same competition as prints.

The Great Recession economy put additional pressure on galleries selling the same prints by an artist, creating online price wars. While this has always gone on, the internet has intensified the competition and rapidly expanded this shift in buying tactics. Smart collectors realize they can shop widely for fine art prints as with everything else, thanks to the convenience of the internet. This is a problem for artists and galleries but, at the same time, an opportunity. It's pure Darwinism.

The survivors are those who learned how to adapt to shifting consumer buying trends. The same will be true for artists.

Formerly, I believed it was bad business for artists to create channel conflict by competing with their galleries unless they were an established name in the industry. It's easy to realize why galleries wouldn't surrender valuable retail space to compete with unknown artists selling the same work on their websites.

In an ideal world, artists and galleries should not have to compete. Unfortunately, it's not such an ideal world and so that's not the case today. Although there is no clear-cut formula for how competing artists or galleries should co-operate, both parties taking the high road is the best approach.

What I mean by the high road for artists is that they need to establish guidelines for what is not only in their best interests, but in the galleries' as well. If you're fortunate enough to have a relationship with a gallery that's moving your work, you should not be in direct competition with them by selling the same images from your website.

Perhaps the gallery markets the originals while you sell the prints, but because each case is unique, there are too many options to explore here. Suffice it to say, it will take creativity and persuasive negotiation to work deals with galleries when you're also selling work on your site or through other distribution channels.

Selling directly to collectors can be a viable marketing decision when you're a known entity. For example, the premier primitive artist, Jane Wooster Scott, appears to do well selling from her website (www.woosterscott. com), while supporting a dealer network.

In Wooster Scott's case, galleries with Americana collectors want to carry her work, despite the channel conflict, because they know that, due to her reputation and the demand for her work, she sells. It's a business decision for them, just as it is for her company. So, while you can aspire to be able to achieve what Scott has managed, building your reputation and demand for your work may be the better way to go. After all, it makes sense that galleries will steadfastly reject artists without a following who plan to compete with them directly. Who can blame them?

Whatever the case, I do think publishers, artists and galleries need to rethink how they collaborate to create a collector base for the artist. What worked in the past may not function best now or in the future: the shifting buying patterns caused by the internet are at the heart of that.

There has always been some naturally occurring antagonism between some galleries and some artists. It's a marriage of sorts. Some are rocky relationships while others are solid; artists feel galleries don't do enough for them, and galleries think artists aren't loyal, are withholding better pieces and ready to jump to the next gallery, and so it goes.

Of course, there also are wonderful stories of galleries and artists sharing blissful success in long-term relationships. However, I've also heard artists ask, with a sneer, in what other business do retailers get their product for free and then Keystone it (100% price increase) when it's sold. On the other hand, I've also heard gallerists lament that it costs them $100 or more per month, per piece on display in rent, not including other expenses such as commissions, benefits, taxes, utilities, advertising and more – and all with no appreciation of their overhead from the artists they serve.

Galleries often rightly find many artists clueless when it comes to understanding the difficulty of creating a collector. But artists often find that galleries fail in adequately representing them and living up to the spirit of their sales and marketing agreements. This is neither a condemnation of either artists or galleries nor of their actions. Everybody puts self-interest first, which is natural. As I said earlier, there's a Darwinian quality to the relationship.

Having said that, this is not the time for either side to be working against the other. The best outcome would be for all parties to realize that, if they don't find a way to cooperate better and deal with the disruptive changes caused by the internet, they'll all suffer in the end.

My advice is as follows: If you're an artist, you need a website. You'll have to figure out how to use it to serve your own needs and that of the galleries or publishers who carry your work, depending on your own particular circumstances. If you're a gallery owner and you're not set up to sell online – and don't plan to be – then start thinking about what your next career will be because you'll soon be an observer in this business, watching the erosion of your sales to your online competitors.

Website Options for Artists

When you start your investigating, you'll find many options for getting a website for your art business. Here are the most common options:

- generic Do-It-Yourself (DIY) site-builder programs that use built-in templates and color schemes provided by the hosting company
- template and semi-custom websites created specifically for artists
- websites built by you, or by someone you know, using Dreamweaver or some other web-building software
- custom websites constructed by a web developer or web development company
- content management systems (CMS), including popular freeware programs such as WordPress, Joomla and Drupal.

Newbies will be tempted by the numerous "free" options available. Unfortunately, most free sites look amateurish and send the wrong message about how seriously you take your career and your art if you use one. You can find free sites from your ISP and other sources, but you get what you pay for, so it's best to forget this approach. On such free websites, users usually have to put up with ads and banners unrelated to your art, and from which you derive no income. It winds up looking like a tacky way to display your artwork and you as a professional. Avoid these temptations to cut corners on investing in your career.

Some web developer companies focus on visual artists. Use your favorite search engine to query for the search term "websites for artists" to find a good representation. Look at as many as necessary to understand your options and corresponding requirements.

Website for Artists Services

- artistwebsite.org
- artsites.ca
- artspan.com
- artstorefronts.com
- artstudiosonline.com
- bigblackbag.com
- faso.com
- foliolink.com
- foliotwist.com
- heavybubble.com
- impactfolios.com
- otherpeoplespixels.com
- scotstyle.com
- sitewelder.com
- smugmug.com (for photographers)

This list is a starting point. Ask around, use the search engines and dig in to find the best choice for your needs.

You should take the time to compare website providers for services and pricing by examining examples of how they feature their artists' works. You might be tempted to contact the artists represented on those sites for their opinions of the services provided, but they might find it burdensome responding to such unsolicited requests. It's easy enough to learn how long an artist has been represented by a particular vendor. Together with the information you glean from inspecting your potential provider's websites, this should be sufficient to help you choose a supplier. Of course, word of mouth is still one of the most reliable sources for suggestions on any services.

Your other options are to construct a site yourself using Dreamweaver or some similar site-building software or to have a site built for you by a developer. The drawback to the first option is that you have to take the time to learn how to create one, and you may not have any training on website or graphic design. You may also need to learn HTML, CSS and PHP. Having a custom site built for you has potential problems if you run into issues with the developer.

Nonetheless, the upside to building your own website from scratch is that you have full control over the entire process. You make all the decisions, from layout, navigation and color schemes, to fonts and more. You'll know how your site works, and you'll be able to make changes without having to rely on a third party.

Instead of building entirely from scratch, you could choose instead to use a type of CMS (content management system) software. The most common are WordPress, Joomla and Drupal, although more are available. WordPress is the most popular as it powers about 25% of the all the sites on the web. Due to the size of the user base, there are more options for building and managing a WordPress site.

WordPress and the other open source programs allow you to build a website using themes, components and plug-ins, which means you don't have to know how to code everything to pull your site together. These programs have free and commercially available themes that you can use to hang your site on. The themes typically allow for a high degree of customization.

With the advent of mobile computing, Google has put a premium on page-loading speed. As a result, speed has become more important in Google page-ranking algorithms. Internet professionals have taken notice, as they always do when the search behemoth speaks. You can speed up your site by simplifying page design, but also by using one of the top methods of speeding up a site, a CDN (content delivery network).

A CDN uses a group of web servers distributed across multiple locations to deliver content more efficiently to users. In this system, the server with the fewest network hops or the server with the quickest response time comes up first. The cost of a CDN to a small business is prohibitive, but as your business and online traffic grow, you may find using a CDN pays its way by improving your user's experience, as well as by enhancing your Google Page and keyword rankings. The end result for you – more traffic directed to your website.

Cloudflare.com is a free, easy-to-use CDN service that I recommend. Caching plugins are helpful too. If you're using

WordPress, look at the W3Total Cache or WP-Rocket caching plugin also. Both cache pages locally, which reduces time-consuming, back-and-forth trips from the computer to the internet. If you're not comfortable with this technology, get the help you need.

If you're using WordPress, then you need to back up your site to a separate server not connected to your hosting account. This is mission critical and a "bacon saver" for when bad things happen – such as getting hacked or having a server (and thus your site) crash. Vaultpress by WordPress and BackUp Buddy are probably the most popular backup resources.

You should also look into some security for your WordPress site. iThemes Security plugin is popular. So is the Sucuri.net service. iThemes Security has a free version. Sucuri is a premium service, but well worth its cost if your site gets hacked because it cleans up the mess and restores it for you.

Generic Website Builders

Besides the other options mentioned above, many artists also use one of the generic site-builder systems. With this choice they can construct their website without knowing how or having to use code editing. The proprietary online tools made available by the site builders make building a site easy. The disadvantage is that you cannot export your content to a different service, or download it for a move. You need to save each page to preserve your content and then copy and paste to rebuild the site elsewhere. Research and choose wisely to avoid unpleasant outcomes like these.

Many website builder platforms also offer turnkey e-commerce solutions. They include secure merchant transactions, shipping options and other features to help you sell your art. Expect to find customizable templates, some designed for artists. Some of the most popular website builders are on the list that follows. As ever, it's advisable to do your research because things sometimes change fast:

- squarespace.com
- web.com
- wix.com
- weebly.com
- godaddy.com

E-commerce is discussed in more detail in a future chapter. Depending on your skill level, your budget, your time in learning how to use the various platforms and your interest in dealing with technology will all come into play when making a final decision.

As previously stated, having a website is not an option. That means learning how to manage using one is also not an option. Unless you have a trusted partner to handle building and maintaining your website, you need to put aside any reservations or negative emotions about technology and websites and get the training and knowledge to create a functional site. With all the choices you have, there is one that will work for you. Bring a positive attitude and an open willingness to learn new things and you will create a website that makes you proud.

Self-Representing and Print-and-Fulfill Websites

In addition to getting your own website, in your own name, established, you can show your work on many other websites. Keep in mind, these other sites showcase a collection of artists and so they're not all about you. While participating in some of them can be worthwhile, regularly review your results and participation after you have your own site up and running. If no results are forthcoming, consider minimizing your exposure on those sites. Having your name and contact information available on them is good for your exposure, so you may want to keep your presence even though your activity is limited.

Since this discussion also concerns the print market, you'll find fewer sites selling reproductions as opposed to original art. Still, the numbers are daunting and the choices many.

These sites sell art prints:

- traditional online e-commerce vendors such as art.com and allposters.com
- print-and-fulfill platforms such as fineartamerica.com, zazzle.com, redbubble.com, artistrising.com, imagekind.com, cafepress.com and deviantart.com

These sites, where typically the artist ships the work to the buyer after the sale, sell originals:

- auction sites such as eBay.com and overstock.com
- artist community websites, such as ebsqart.com and artflock. com
- artist promotional sites where you upload images to a gallery and fulfill upon sale such as artspan.com, yessy.com, artbyus.com and picassomio.com
- juried sites including saatchiart.com, ugallery.com, artfulhome.com, artthatfits.com, paddle8.com and too many more to name
- brick-and-mortar galleries that sell prints through their websites such as XanaduGallery.com

The above represent the broad categories of places where you can sell your art online. If you do enough searching, you'll find other varieties of sites among the many that sell art prints. To give you an example of the breadth of the online art gallery market, the ArtsyShark.com website first published a list of 125 places to sell your art online. As you can tell by looking at its URL for the page with the listings (http://www.artsyshark.com/125-places-to-sell/), the list has since doubled to 250 places to sell your art online.

From my observation and research, few artists, if any, make a living by selling through online sites. Some artists are known to have done well marketing their art on eBay. On that site Michel Keck (keckfineart.com) reportedly earned an average of $20,000 per month, with a high peak gross of $42,000 in one single month. Times have changed since her early successes. I don't know how her sales and site are doing in 2016.

It's worth noting that around 2006, eBay lost many top sellers, including Keck and Natasha Wescoat. Ten years late, in 2016, Etsy.com made changes to its terms for artists that caused consternation and abandonment of the site. Things change, but you have little or no control over these sites. Use them but never come to rely on them, and you'll always be okay.

Most of the sites mentioned here have membership fees, some with a free basic membership and premium services for a fee. You'll need to perform your own due diligence to determine which, if any, sites are viable for expanding your art sales. Some, such as The Artful Home, are juried. In that case, you'll need to apply to be accepted and sold through such venues.

The abrupt closing of the Boundless Gallery in early 2010 offers some insight into how online gallery markets can be gone in a blink. Boundless reported only that, although the business was not bankrupt, it was not generating enough profit to make the venture worthwhile. This news came as quite a shock to the artists who'd invested their time in promoting their work through the site. I'm surmising that none of them were making a full-time living from it but also that some were financially hurt by the closing.

The sad tale of Boundless Gallery leads to one of my deepest convictions about prospects for long-term success for artists in the print market. It confirms my opinion that artists should do everything they can to control as many different distribution channels as possible. To varying degrees, this goes for all artists these days, on nearly every level – but especially those in the print market. That means becoming self-reliant and selling direct.

I do not advocate abandoning sites that sell art. Many of them offer excellent programs that can help an artist make more sales and grow awareness for them and their art. In fact, it's still worthwhile to investigate and get involved with as many as possible, but only after doing the proper research. At the least, each site's results are searchable, and it's likely your name will rank higher on some of them than on your own site. Steady blogging and proper SEO on your own website can change this result.

In the long run, it's your career – and it's your responsibility to manage it. The more you rely on others' resources to market and sell your art, the more vulnerable you are to decisions beyond your control that shut down those sales. When you sell direct and build meaningful personal relationships with your collectors, you give yourself the best odds of sustaining your career through the ups and downs of the overall economy and of surviving the changes in the marketplace.

Search Engine Optimization (SEO) for Artists

Your website must be attractive not only to your visitors but also to search engines. To be successful at SEO, you or your webmaster will spend considerable time and energy to create:

- human-readable URLs

- XML sitemaps
- keyword-rich alt and title tags
- deep-linking architecture, internal links within your site
- W3-compliant code
- on-page search engine optimization
- inbound links.

There is more to SEO than the above items, but if you manage each of them, you're well on your way to gaining high page rankings from Google and other search engines. Start by exploring your favorite search engine to learn more about the bullet points above. Search for each one individually and study the results. Then search for "SEO for artists" to find specifics for your art-based website.

Learn to think in "keyword phrases" when it comes to creating copy for your site. You don't want it to be a bunch of copy-pasted, unintelligible gobbledygook or clichés. It should read in a natural, unforced language that contains the keywords and phrases that will facilitate searches. For instance, never use a generic "click here" text link when you could be linking with a keyword phrase such as "still life paintings" or "photorealism prints."

Search engines are about one thing: relevance. It's the goal of a search engine to return the most relevant results to every query. Keep this in mind as you work on making your site as SEO-friendly as possible. Dead links are unfriendly and a search engine no-no. You'll be dinged (dropped in search engine page ranking) for having broken or dead links on your site. Search, and you'll find numerous broken link checkers available.

Metadata, including the title, description, meta tags and keywords, are crucial to SEO success. Matt Cutts is a senior software engineer for Google and is also the face of Google on YouTube. You can watch YouTube videos featuring Matt Cutts to find informative and useful videos that take the mystery out of the algorithms that Google and other search engines use. To that end, you might also subscribe to the Google Webmaster Channel. You will find a growing list of more than 200 informative and useful videos aimed at de-mystifying Google's vaunted search algorithms and SEO in general.

One thing you'll learn from Cutts is that Google does not in-dex keywords in metadata, the information viewed by search engines rather than by website visitors. While higher Google ranking is the primary target for all SEO activity, other search engines do matter, and some of them do still index keywords in metadata, so writing with keywords in mind is still worthwhile.

Pay-Per-Click (PPC) Advertising

Employing SEO tactics will help your site rank higher in or-ganic or natural searches in which users type in what they regard as the keywords for the search they're undertaking. Those links and their order are the coin of the realm, the Holy Grail of the search being an inclusion at the top of the list. The non-organic search, on the other hand, produces the results you see on a page, results that consist primarily of pay-per-click advertising.

Since Google owns a dominant portion of online search, its AdWords program is the most popular source of paid advertising. You can use its Search-Based Keyword Tool (www.google.com/sktool/#) to help identify the best keywords and keyword phrases most appropriate for optimizing your site and to find the best keywords to bid on in AdWords and other paid advertising programs. My advice is to work at getting your site optimized as much as possible before considering the PPC alternative.

Should you decide to pursue it, spend the time to study how PPC – especially AdWords – works before you start because you can waste a lot of money learning what *not* to do with an unfocused and amateur AdWords campaign. You'll find Microsoft and Yahoo return fewer results, for instance, but also that you'll spend less money on them during the learning curve. Facebook and Myspace also offer versions of PPC advertising. You may want to look into their programs if you plan to pursue this form of advertising.

Local Search

Statistics show that somewhere in the neighborhood of 79% of households do some kind of search for a local product or service on a daily basis. On that basis, it's safe to say that many of your best prospects are searching for local artists using the internet rather than the Yellow Pages or other more "traditional" means. Major search engines, in fact, are competing to replace your local phone book. Obviously then, it's important to get your business listed online to take advantage of the growing number of people using a local search.

As a visual artist, you're likely seeking a broader audience on the internet than just in your local market, although by no means should you be ignoring the "locals." I have a blog post titled "Local Search for the Local Artist – Grow Where You Are Planted" in which you can find information on the Art Marketing News blog. It extols the virtues of building a homegrown following.

Getting listed in local search engines also helps create more quality backlinks to your site, cross-references of sorts which connect to links on other websites that make reference to your site. You want to make sure you stake your claim on the "Google 10-pack." When you search for a term such as "fine artist Phoenix, AZ," you want to be included in the 10 listings beside the map on Google's first page of results. On his www.Expand2Web.com site, Don Campbell offers tutorials on how to use local search.

You'll want to start with the top three local search engines:

- Google Local Business Center – www.google.com/lbc
- Yahoo Local – http://listings.local.yahoo.com/csubmit/index.php
- Microsoft (Bing) – https://ssl.bing.com/listings/ListingCenter.aspx

But don't stop with the big three local search engines. Get yourself listed in every local, regional and national directory you can find. All of them are eager for listings – it's how they become and stay relevant. You shouldn't have to pay for this service as most are happy to have your listing and for an opportunity to pitch paid services to you.

Your list should include the Yellow Pages, White Pages, cable company listings and local search engines, such as Scottsdale.com. If you search for "directory listings your town," you'll find dozens of places to include in your free listings.

If you haven't concentrated on the local market, you should. There's common sense to this approach, not unlike the "Think globally, act locally" campaign. For one thing it's easier to make local contacts and develop small business and media connections first. What's more, you can improve sales and increase your local "footprint" by eliminating shipping charges and even including hanging services. The greater your local presence, the better your odds of earning a larger share of a broader market.

Common Sense Ideas to Promote Your Business:

- Include your URL on everything you print or email, including on letterhead and business cards, and in email signatures.
- Create or purchase promotional items. Mini prints, greeting cards, coffee mugs and T-shirts are beautiful items and provide a regular reminder to visit your site.

- Include your website address in every directory listing you make.

- Get a magnetic sign or a back window graphic with your website address.

- Launch a sweepstake to offer anyone who registers on your site – or anyone who subscribes to e-newsletters within a particular time frame – the chance to win or receive a free gift.

- Add a resources page to your website and use it to create your own link exchange by asking sites complementary to yours to swap links. Keep the links relevant and check to make sure your link is being posted on the cooperating site.

- Become active by commenting in online discussion groups, chats and blogs, and always include your URL in your signature. Be polite, and don't spam with unwanted messages. Make sure your comments add value.

- Put an "email this link" on every page of your site.

- Create a survey to help you determine what your customers want and what they like.

- Use online classified advertising and online auction sites such as Craigslist.org and eBay.com to increase exposure to your site and products.

Site Submission and Statistics

Search engine crawlers will eventually find your site without help. However, don't take that they will for granted. You should submit your site yourself or pay a service to do it for you. Numerous sites offer to help you with search engine submission for free.

Many of these sites also provide other tools to assist you with keyword density, meta tag generation, checking broken links and link popularity. The tradeoff for free service is that you agree to receive their marketing messages on your site. Nonetheless, using all of the named services will help you make sure your site is toned up as much as possible.

You need to know the "who, what, when and why" of your website visitors. Once again, Google has an excellent free resource to help with this, called the Google Analytics tool (www.google.com/analytics).

As you begin to use your statistics to understand how traffic is arriving at your site, you can then apply it to making smart choices in online advertising. You can also use the information to write blog posts based on the keywords that generate the most traffic to your site. As the saying goes, "Knowledge is power."

If you blog frequently and authoritatively, search engines will take note. Having an active blog is arguably the best SEO tool in your online marketing arsenal. So, if you don't have a blog, consider starting one!

Content

Because your website is a personal reflection of you and your work, keeping it updated with compelling content is a key to maintaining your credibility and gaining repeat visits to your site.

Updating includes proactively addressing visitors' questions and concerns. You can also help ease any anxiety buyers have about doing business with a new online marketer. You do that by incorporating the following essentials into your website:

- Include both the company and owner's name with complete address.
- Have an About Us tab/page since that's typical among the most visited information on a website. When I go to a new site and I'm not familiar with the owner or the business, I head straight to the About Us page for more details.
- Include testimonials from actual collectors to generate a human touch and attract potential clients.
- Include a FAQ. If you get repeat questions, then provide clear answers as a service to your visitors and you. Make things easier for everyone.
- List the products used in creating your work.
- Explain shipping policies. Who takes the risk of transportation damage or loss? Is shipping insurance included?
- Post a return policy. A reasonable suggestion is seven days from the receipt of the painting/artwork with a 100% refund.
- Be straightforward about what you offer and your terms.
- Include a privacy policy, especially if you intend to ask for any kind of information from visitors/buyers.

Be sure to have an SSL certificate. It's required for a merchant account and shopping cart. If you collect any kind of personal data in a form on your site, including just asking for name and email address, you need one.

Alyson Stanfield, the Art Biz Coach, provides insight into writing an About Us page. She says you need to inject personality into your About page, and I agree. This is a chance to let your personality – as well as your accomplishments – shine through. A dry recitation of facts about where you were born and went to school or the accolades you've collected along the way just doesn't cut it.

In addition to using this page for bragging rights, give your readers a glimpse at your life beyond being an artist. What other passions do you have? Do you love to cook? Are you addicted to the Project Runway TV show? Are you a closet or unabashed fan of American Idol? Do you belong to non-art-related groups? Do you play an instrument, sing, dance or act? Do you have a partner in your business that makes it go for you? Are you an avid poker player, NASCAR fan, or college or pro sports fanatic?

Don't be shy about including amusing or interesting items from your life history. It can make your prospects and collectors feel more connected to you. So if you've been a firefighter, fallen in a tub of holy water or met your wife on American Airlines – wait, that's me! – you can connect on levels beyond an appreciation of your creativity (yours and theirs). I like writing in the first person – Hi there. It's Barney – and find it stiff to write in the third. Whatever you choose, be consistent. Otherwise, you'll just confuse your visitors.

When it comes to writing web content, it's a good idea to get professional help. Good copywriters can make a huge difference in your presentation. They'll use your words and style and help you polish your copy and, equally important, make sure you're using good keyword-rich phrases to help with your SEO.

Contact information should not be just a submittal form. Those forms are not entirely reliable. When I find a site with no physical address, phone number and regular email, it sends up flares. I always wonder what someone's hiding, or if they're arrogant or incompetent. Whatever that site is offering has to be very compelling for me to go further, let alone to return.

Under-construction homepages are okay if that's all you have ready during site development. Otherwise, don't use them and avoid having links to pages with an annoying nothing but "Coming Soon." Besides, it makes you look amateurish. Be respectful of your visitors' time and patience: remove links that go nowhere.

Include your prices. People shopping on the internet expect convenience. If you make them dig too deeply or contact you directly for that information, they'll likely go someplace more user-friendly (I've included more on this topic later in the book.)

Gathering Email Addresses and Privacy

In the past, I emphasized the importance of building a dealer network, and while it's still crucial, your new horizons should include building a direct following with your collectors and fans. Working on your target audiences should be a daily ritual. One of your most vital tasks is to be consistently focused on harvesting email addresses from those interested in your work.

Despite the justified clamor about spam, you'll be pleased with and surprised by how many people will still trust you with their email address when you promise not to use it for any other purpose but to contact them about your work. To accomplish that end, you should have a privacy statement with a clearly visible link to it on your website. Further, you should clearly state that you promise never to share or sell the email addresses you collect. You can find help to create a privacy statement at http://www.freeprivacypolicy.com.

Having a link to a privacy statement on your website will make you stand out as professional and courteous. It's also a reassurance you can refer to when you're attempting to collect email addresses. If people know you have a posted privacy policy, it is just one more reason for them to trust you with their email addresses.

Navigation and Design

Your site can have a stunning visual design, but if that beautiful display doesn't convert browsers into buyers or generate leads, it's dysfunctional. Your visitors need to be able to navigate effortlessly within your website to the information they're looking for. They also need to understand precisely what other goods and services are available.

Make it simple to find things. Keep related items in relevant categories. If you paint and sculpt, don't bury your sculpture on some obscure link deep within the site. Put it in a separate category on the home page, along with whatever else you have to offer.

When it comes to a website design, whether someone is doing it for you or you're doing it yourself, the layout and functionality of the site are vastly significant. I've seen some artist websites with 10 different sloppily organized online galleries or portfolios. This forces buyers to move from one portfolio to the next, which is an easy, quick way to lose your web visitor's attention. Another sin is not providing some sort of search function on your site if it's dense or layered and has a large number of images on display. Having no search function makes it difficult for users to navigate the site and to find everything the artist has on display.

I recommend you set a limit of 50 pieces on your site. More than that is overwhelming. Also, show only your best pieces. If you're going to show pieces online that are also available in a brick-and-mortar gallery, don't sell them direct to the customer unless you're planning to give the gallery its full commission. Otherwise, insert a link to the gallery's website and clearly explain that this is where customers can purchase that piece. As mentioned before, transparency is a key to success with your online marketing.

One piece of feedback I've heard again and again from clients selling online is that they're astonished by how quickly their products sell once I update their sitemap and add some simple searches which break down their work into categories. They also tell me that products they'd struggled to sell for ages are now moving from those new categories.

To better understand website dynamics involved here, consider the 8-second test. Maybe you've heard of it. Research indicates that this is the time limit your website has to make a first impression on visitors – what marketing gurus refer to as the FMOT (the first moment of truth). To win in such a speed-dating marketplace, the graphics you choose are important, but even more so is the bold headline you write. Use it to give your visitors an exciting and compelling reason to stay on *your* site. This may be contrary to the advice you may have been provided by a web designer but, while pictures, graphics and logos each have their place, they cannot replace a strong opening headline.

Coming up with a bold headline that contains a definite promise or benefit is how you arrest the attention of casual web surfers and begin to convert them to customers. In other words, spend the time to succinctly tell me the principal reason why I should choose to do business with you. There's a fine line between puffery and efficient promotion. Dial it in and win.

This information is not to be construed a primer on creating compelling website copy. As mentioned above, if writing compelling copy isn't your strong suit, you may be well served in finding a professional copywriter. Yes, it costs money to hire good help, but when you think about how important it is to create an active website, it's worth the investment. Your website will tirelessly sell for you, 24/7. It can open doors like no other medium. When well done, it will be your single most valuable marketing tool.

Every page on your website should exist for a reason. Starting with a compelling, benefit-oriented headline, each page should follow with a strong paragraph that supports the headline and draws the readers' interest. The goal is to arrest their attention first, and then involve them further and, finally, to present them with a call to action. That's a challenge, but it's worth doing. After all, it's how you'll make your site a success. You've got to get past the 8-second, FMOT (first moment of truth) test.

Your site is more than a virtual mall or electronic brochure. It's a means of lead generation unlike any other, reflecting an unspoken internet quid pro quo. If you expect your visitors to respond to your call to action – by giving you their names or buying something – you'll get the best response when you give them something of value in return.

I previously provided examples of how Hazel Dooney and Banksy offered free, high-quality digital downloads of their work. There's nothing wrong in following their example. After all, it worked. As with a headline, the more time you spend crafting a good offer, the better your results. The same goes for buyers. How about giving any customer a free mini print, a pack of gift cards or free shipping on the first order?

CHAPTER 4

E-commerce

If you do build a great experience, customers tell each other about that. Word of mouth is very powerful. – Jeff Bezos

I believe artists who do not have e-commerce enabled on their websites today are missing the boat. Having the ability to sell art directly from your website and/or blog is a terrific way to establish your tireless 24-hour sales system on the internet. You may not have grand plans for selling scores of art online, which is okay, but by not selling any, you're missing an easy opportunity to make more money.

Some people like to buy direct from a website with no human interaction. Why discourage them? Others take more interaction. But once you get your site up and running you might find you have a knack for e-commerce, or that your art sells well on the internet for a variety of reasons. There simply is no reason you should choose to share direct sales income with another distribution channel when you can drive traffic to your own site and sell direct from it.

There are numerous e-commerce platforms available. Some, like Zen Cart or Open Cart, are free, open-source software programs that can be installed on a server or shared hosting account. However, both seem to have fallen out of favor in recent years. WooCommerce is the most popular -commerce solution for WordPress. However, that, does not mean it's the only, or even the best one. As always, you need to research to find the best option for your business.

There are standalone e-commerce sites. In an ever changing landscape, Shopify has grown to be considered among the best generic shopping cart options for artists who don't want to deal with WordPress and plugins and all the updates and maintenance they require.

Don't stop here with the Shopify and WooCommerce suggestions. In your favorite search engine, enter the term, "e-commerce software," and you'll find many possibilities. Naturally, some are more expensive than others. Doing your own research is the way to get the best results with the least aggravation.

The alternative is to use one of the previously listed generic and artist-specific website builders. Many of them do an excellent job and provide additional marketing resources, as well. The internet and social media offer you easy options to ask questions of other artists to learn what they're using, what they like and don't like, and to get their recommendations. When you find a consensus and it points to a solution you already felt good about, you'll have dialed in the one that's best for you.

Should You Price Your Art on Your Website?

Some artists question the effectiveness of including pricing on their website. I firmly believe you should show your prices. Consumers are using the internet because they want the ease of buying online. If they must contact you by email, or worse, have to call you or submit a contact form to find out how much something costs, I guarantee you are losing sales. You're not going to convince people to buy if they have to take extra steps.

What's more, when potential buyers can't find your prices, that raises questions about your reasons. Are you too important to put them on your work? Are you forcing shoppers to contact you for a sales pitch? Are the prices left off so you can play "Let's make a deal"? But If you think "blatant" pricing harms the presentation of your art, then include a pricing grid on a separate, easily accessed page where a visitor can learn what things cost without having either to leave the site or call or email you.

If you're not attaching prices because your pricing is inconsistent, then you have a different problem. One you can easily fix by committing to standardized pricing on your images across all your distribution channels. In this age, you need to be authentic and transparent, or you ultimately will lose customers and gallery support because of your inconsistencies.

Being consistent with your pricing is the fair and ethical way to treat your collectors and your galleries, and you. Unless desperate, why would you cut your prices? Doing so takes money out of your pocket and in most cases devalues your art. Do not make the mistake of not valuing your marketing costs in time and money. A primary reason artists undercut prices is because they fail to factor the marketing, inventory and labor costs into creating their work. If you don't respect your prices, why should anyone else?

Many artists who sell online fail in the area of shipping, ordering and returns. You need to be abundantly clear about how you handle those elements of digital marketing. You want to make the experience ordering from you as easy as possible for your customers, so when quoting a price, be sure to include the cost of shipping and handling, and explain your return policy. These things are all part of the online buying experience.

User Experience is Critical to Success

The easier it is for someone to find a piece of art, navigate the checkout procedure and finalize the purchase online, the likelier you are to get the sale and not have an abandoned shopping cart on your site. I cannot tell you how many times I've abandoned a shopping cart because finding the full price, including shipping, was too complicated. I don't want to be required to give you all my contact information just to get a price. Let me give you my Zip Code and you provide the full price, including shipping. At that point, if the price is right and I wish to buy, I'll give you all the required information to complete the sale.

Use Your Shipping Methods as a Promotional Tool

I suggest you upload a video or slideshow on your blog and on your website that shows how your art is packed for shipping. In it you'll want to show someone in a clean area, with white gloves, handling the art carefully, putting it into the shipping container and closing it, so your customers can see how much respect you have for the art that you're shipping to them. This is just another way to present yourself as a high-level professional. One who appreciates your art and your customers. This is so easy to do. If you use a video, post on YouTube where you can get more traffic and links back to your site or blog. Because YouTube ranks second only to Google for search engine traffic, you should utilize it as much as possible. Having a shipping video is just one smart way to do it.

Mobile Responsive Sites

The strong trend is for consumers to use mobile devices over desktops and laptops. Because of that trend, your site needs to be responsive. That means it will have to shrink to fit on the smallest cell phone but still have all your content visible and your navigation easy to follow and use.

If you want visitors to come to your site and stay, you have to make it a pleasant experience for them. Having to find and use scroll bars is a sure way to get rid of your site visitors fast.

Online Galleries and Online Art Venues

If you feel confused by the sheer number of sites offering to sell your art, you're normal. There are literally thousands of them attempting to sell art online. They range from the pure e-commerce poster and print market (represented by industry leader art.com and its sister site, allposters.com) to local or regional sites that represent a few artists from any defined geographical area.

Sites such as saatchiart.com, ugallery.com and even amazon.com/art all offer artists free traffic. However, free traffic creates intense competition for attention. With so many artists and so many visitors you cannot build a business plan based on selling to buyers who've just "found" you online. While you'll get some sales this way, they'll be unpredictable, so you won't be able to rely on a steady income from them.

As an artist, you can certainly take advantage of a gallery with a large and established online presence by agreeing to have it sell your art on its website. In those situations, and to avoid any potential conflicts, you need to inquire of the online gallery management whether you can list a piece on your own site and their site at the same time. If you're any kind of prolific artist, you should have enough work to spread it around, especially if you're a print artist and offer reproductions of your artwork.

Advice for Best Results When Selling Art Online

No matter which of the methods you choose to get your art online, following these guidelines will help you make more sales:

- Keep marketing offline. You should not make your online store the only means of getting your art sold. Think of each as complementing the other. They are both distribution channels that need your attention.
- When using an online gallery or artist marketplace, know your rights. Don't take anything for granted. Read policies, and terms and conditions thoroughly. If you don't understand something, ask for clarification so you know what it means. Keep copies of any correspondence. It's up to you to know how you'll be paid and when. You need to be aware of any guards or protection the site offers you.
- Make your contact information available on every page, and be sure to respond to all inquiries as soon as possible. If you can't be there 24/7, use an auto-responder email to explain your hours of operation and offer a timeframe for expected responses, such as within 24 hours. If you are using online galleries, realize not all attract the same demographics. Research to learn the profiles of the typical buyers and use that information to adjust what you offer on the site.

- Create the ambiance you would like as a visitor. Think about your design and your user's experience. The more you can recreate the feel of a beautiful art gallery, if that's what you're after, the more comfortable and welcome your site visitors will feel.

Never forget that online selling is a process. Every step takes you closer to making more sales. Building your list, building your website and getting traffic to it takes time. If you commit to your success and stay focused on doing your best to do those three things, you'll generate the sales that will fuel your career for the long haul.

Selling on Social Media

There have been numerous attempts for social media platforms, notably Facebook, to allow its users to create an online store within those platforms. As of 2016, none have had wild success. Some have been abysmal failures. I believe Facebook will continue to refine its efforts to make online sales possible. If you see a choice that looks worthy and useful to you, give it a try. Just always remember you do not want to come to rely on sales through third-party sites as your primary source of income.

CHAPTER 5

Domain Names

O, be some other name! What's in a name? That which we call a rose By any other name would smell as sweet. – Shakespeare

Perhaps it's the colors of your art that catches your buyers' attention. Maybe it's the medium. It's the same with the Internet. You need a "hook" to grab the web surfers' interest, and that comes down to the name you choose for your site

Technically speaking, a domain name is a unique alphanumeric name that identifies individual websites on the internet. It's the human-readable alternative to the octet series of numbers that make up an IP (Internet Protocol) address.

Still, an understanding of the basics is essential. A domain can be any length up to 67 characters and made of the 26 letters of the English alphabet, numbers 0 to 9, and hyphens (-). You cannot begin or end a domain with a hyphen, but you can include multiple hyphens. Domain names have a TLD (top level domain) suffix or extension. While more are added regularly, the most common suffixes include .com, .net, .org, .biz, .info, .us. There are now boutique extensions for such things as .gallery, .art, and .media, for example. I will take a longer name with a shorter .com over any of these other options any day. My smartphone has a .com key. That says it all.

A Matter of Ownership

Don't let any company hold your domain name for you. Insist on having your domain in an account you control. It's a question of ownership. There's no reason a web developer or anyone else needs to have *your* domain in *their* account. It would be tragic if you lost your website because your designer skipped out on you, went broke or took it down in a disagreement.

You cannot overestimate the value of your domain name; you can, however, rebuild a website. In the worst case scenario, if you lose access to your site or if it comes down without your consent, you can still restore it *if you own your domain name*. It's not nearly so easy to rebrand yourself and your website if you lose that name – or if you never ever had control of it in the first place.

If you're having a website custom built, one that requires shared hosting or a server, you should have the hosting account in your name and under your control for the reasons I indicated earlier. It ultimately comes down to ownership.

You can always set up the web developer with hosting account executive status, FTP access or some other arrangement that doesn't take ultimate control from you. Naturally, if you're using a full-service provider that specializes in artist websites, you won't be able to exercise such control of the hosting. But, remember – there's never a reason not to have a domain name in your own account. Never.

Choosing Your Domain Name

When it comes to your domain name, keep it simple. Choosing the best, the most suitable name is paramount. It will become your online identity, the wordmark of your brand, an essential part of your brand name as an artist and, as such, part of every communication. You'll use it for all your communication. It will be an integral part of your effort to brand your name as an artist.

It may seem obvious, but it's nevertheless worth emphasizing that you should use your name. That's what people remember. Check for yourname.com and register it immediately if it's available. A good source for purchasing domain names is Go Daddy (www.godaddy.com). You'll get a free email address with your registration. I encourage you to use this as your primary business email address.

Don't modify your domain name unless necessary. That is, if you have yourname.com, then stick with it. If you have a common name, it's not likely available, in which case you can consider adding a modifier such as yournameart-ist.com, yournamefineart.com, yournamestudio.com. You get the idea.

Avoid being cute, clever or generic. Using descriptive phrases instead of your name is not a good idea. Terms such as KittyCatArtist.com or GrandCanyonartist.com will not serve you well. Stick with your name and a brief modifier, if necessary.

Domain names are not case-sensitive. In fact, they'll resolve to lower case in the address bar of a web browser. However, you can use uppercase letters to make longer names more readable. For instance, I present my blog as ArtMarketingNews.com to make it easier for the eye to follow and to pronounce.

This leads to the question of what to do if you have years of branding under some domain name that goes against my earlier advice. My blog's a good example. After working to establish it as a high-ranking, authoritative business resource for visual artists, I agonized over losing the momentum and search engine visibility I'd gained under ArtPrintIssues.com, but I took the plunge because the branding was more important than any temporary search engine rankings losses. You may make the same decision for similar reasons. As it turned out, I was able to move to ArtMarketingNews.com more easily than I'd thought possible. I 've never regretted making the change.

For those who may not have had good advice and thus have chosen a name poorly, I wouldn't rule out buying a better domain name. You could begin by redirecting web surfers from your established domain to the new one, with the long-range goal of completely rebranding your website with the new, improved domain name.

Remember, too, that the .com domain is king! The number of .com TLD's swamps all others. There are about three times more .com domains registered than the total of .net, .org, .biz, .info and .us combined. We're conditioned to think .com, even though we may have read or heard of some other TLD.

Granted, the chances of obtaining a short, descriptive .com identifier becomes more challenging each day. But, resist the temptation to use one of the other TLDs such as .net or .org for your artist website. If you choose a .net, for instance, and there's another similar .com domain, you can be sure you'll send traffic to it. Given the predominance of the .com extension, why would you intentionally put yourself at a disadvantage by buying some other name?

Other Considerations

If you live outside the U.S., you may want to consider getting a country code domain name to go with your .com TLD. For instance, if you live in Great Britain, you may want to promote yourself within your country as yournameartist.co.uk. Should you choose this route, you create more challenges and decisions over which to use in different situations? You could direct users who access the country code domain to your .com site as any easy fix.

There is a school of thought that to protect your domain name's intellectual property value, you should purchase the name with the other popular TLDs, such as .net, .org., .biz, .us and .info. Since this tactic can add considerably to your marketing budget, I believe you'd more likely do better to buy more years of marketing for your .com website. Should your name be easily misspelled, however, you'd do well to purchase the obvious misspellings and forward those domains to your primary domain name.

Using hyphens allows you to claim the same generic name as someone else who has previously registered the name. But I recommend against using something such as your-name-artist.com. It will be confusing to users, it's harder to type, and you'll end up sending traffic to the non-hyphenated site. Also, you 'll wind up spending time, energy and money to educate your collectors just to insert the hyphen.

Naturally, make sure you're not violating copyrights. You can check to see if a name is trademarked at the U.S. Copyright Office (www.copyright.gov/ records). It can be costly to have to start over again, and even more to have to defend yourself against a lawsuit.

Just because domain names can up to 67 characters doesn't mean you should use as many characters as possible. Shorter is better, with four or five syllables being optimal. If you do opt for a longer name, make sure it's keyword rich. Don't use slang or incorporate anything trendy that will be dated in a couple of years. If you're using more than your name, set expectations with your choice so that, when your domain name is heard, it instantly and accurately conveys the type of content to be found on your site.

You can use a whois lookup service, such as Ajax Whois (www.ajaxwhois.com), to research available domains more quickly. If you find a name that you want, but one that's already taken, you can try to buy it from its owner. Be prepared to pay a premium for an existing domain, especially if it has a website attached to it. There is domain appraisal services and domain buying services that can help.

I trust you can see the importance of choosing and using the right domain name. Although the price to own a domain name is small, the impact from it is immense. Besides all of the other aspects discussed here, you should use your domain name in your email communications. It's the smart, professional way to set yourself apart from your competition still using Gmail, AOL and other free accounts. You'll learn more in the next chapter.

CHAPTER 6

Email Marketing for Artists

How to write a good email: 1. Write your email 2. Delete most of it. Send. – Dan Munz

Expanding Your Art Career with Email Marketing

Email marketing is the most affordable and easy way to communicate directly with your prospects, partners, fans and collectors. If you haven't yet embraced the power of email marketing, there's no better time than now to get started.

Begin building an email marketing subscriber list of patrons, fans, friends and followers that you can communicate with on your own terms. To any small business, a responsive email marketing list is a tremendous, tangible bottom-line asset.

Successful Email Marketing for Artists Is Multifaceted

Because growing your list of contact email addresses is a critical component of your art career and email marketing success, I've made it the first topic in this multipart discussion on email marketing for artists.

Who Should Be on Your Email Marketing List?

Your list should include:

- clients and potential clients
- family, friends and fans
- art professionals, including gallery owners, art consultants, art dealers and designers
- business and professional contacts
- centers of influence – mavens and connectors as described by Malcolm Gladwell in his bestseller *The Tipping Point: How Little Things Can Make a Big Difference*

Permission Is Required – Be Respectful

Unlike postal mail, you cannot send mass email without each recipient's permission. It's illegal (see the CAN SPAM Act for details), and everyone hates spam. So don't do it. If you're sending email to Canadians, even from outside Canada, you must abide by CASL (Canada's anti-spam legislation).

Unless you have a trusted personal relationship with someone, do not add their name to your list no matter how promising and tempting it might be. Business cards casually collected and email addresses found on the internet don't give you permission to add someone's address to your email marketing list.

You can send a single, personalized email to someone who's not on your list. However, even if that recipient replies, you can't add that person to your email marketing list without permission. Make sure all your emails include an easy-to-use opt-out link.

Growing Your Email Marketing List

Capturing email addresses requires your ongoing attention. If you work to make it an ingrained daily habit, your list will grow fast. There are many opportunities for you to collect email addresses.

Your website, blog, newsletter, email signature and social media are among the most useful. With them, you can include an enticing web form or link to make it easy to join your list. All email marketing service providers offer web forms to enable quick, painless sign-ups to your list.

Just remember to ask for permission to add someone when exchanging information during in-person encounters. A good practice is to follow up immediately with a thank you, with a reminder to each one about that inclusion. Auto-responders are ideal for this purpose. I'll cover them in a later discussion.

Digital Email Marketing List-Building Tips

Add a form or link to each page of your website and to posts on your blog.

In your regular emails, add a link in your signature line to invite recipients to join your email marketing list. When you send something to your list, include both a "forward me" and a "sign up" feature in your e-newsletters, announcements and other messages.

Place your sign-up form on your Facebook page, or use a prominent link to a hosted web form. Do the same with a link in your Twitter profile. If you participate in other social media such as Pinterest or LinkedIn, do some Google searches to explore how to leverage your presence there for building your email list.

Offline Email Marketing List-Building Suggestions

High visibility opportunities for growing email marketing lists for artists are gallery shows, art shows and tradeshows. Also, presentations and public speaking give you an easy way to collect email addresses. Take the time to tell attendees what they'll receive for subscribing so they'll know what to expect from your messages.

At your art fair or festival booth, place a mailing list sign-up sheet on one of your tables. Use bright signage to attract attention. Include a link to your email marketing list form on your business cards, brochures, flyers and postcards.

Use a URL shortener to make an easy-to-remember personalized link. I use x.co/barney for my Art Marketing News email-marketing list.

Give a Little, Get a Lot

It's a fact that if you give people something, they're much more inclined to give back to you. Entice your email marketing list prospects with an offer or a gift. Some suggestions are exclusive discounts, offers to join your fan club with advance notice on new images and products, invitations to private-showing parties, free shipping, or free hanging/installation for local collectors.

If you're in the print market, offer mini prints or note cards. Partner with a frame shop to offer discounts from that shop. You could do the same with a local restaurant looking for new customers, especially if it's one where you have your art displayed. Use your own creativity on your list to come up with unique ways to encourage participation.

Be Proactive, Take the Lead, Enjoy the Benefits

You can offer to trade lists with other artists or other businesses. That means, for example, that you would agree to send an email to your list promoting the frame shop's business and the shop would do likewise for your art business.

There are endless creative ways you can work with others to build your list. When you take personal ownership of the process and the lead in working with others to make cooperative arrangements flourish, you are certain to enjoy newfound success. This will extend beyond list-building to other important aspects of your art career.

Quality Beats Quantity

Your mailing list doesn't have to be huge to be effective. It's more important to have a responsive list that helps you develop deeper relationships with your subscribers. Your email marketing list is powerful. One with a few hundred names can help you pack a gallery with your best prospects at your openings. You can use your email list to drive traffic to your website, or to some event or show where your art will be exhibited.

Make Email List-Building a Top Priority

Building, maintaining and regularly using your list needs to be a high-priority activity. As you build your email marketing list, your contacts will grow, as will your ability to influence them. Don't overlook the tremendous opportunities for building your successful art career by routinely using the effective email marketing tips you learned here.

DIY Email Marketing for Artists Doesn't Pay

Email marketing is not something you want to do on your own. Although you can find software packages to manage an email list and send bulk mailings from your own server, I don't advise that practice. For time, expense, results and legality, DIY program email marketing for artists is not a good fit.

To begin with, bulk mailing triggers spam blockers. That means you must keep your domain name and IP address from being blacklisted by spam-blocking services. If that happens, you'll find *all* of your email, both individual and mass messages, blocked. Your Internet Service Provider (ISP) also may cut off your email service. And, your desktop bulk mail sender will not have an automated opt-out link.

Also, not all your subscribers are set up or want to receive email in HTML format, which allows for images, text formatting, background color and so forth. Your email marketing service will give you the option to create both HTML and text formats, a function most desktop bulk mailer software does not support.

The software an email marketing service uses detects the type (HTML or text) your subscriber uses, then delivers the correct version. An HTML version sent to a text editor will look terrible, so just don't do it.

Options for Email Marketing for Artists

Nevertheless, to succeed in your art marketing efforts, you do need an effective email marketing program. Fortunately, you have a choice of many such programs with a variety of options, which makes choosing the best one a challenge. Virtually all email marketing service companies offer affordable, easy-to-use bulk email services. You can use them to communicate with collectors, fans, dealers and prospects with a professional and legal system.

How Much Do Email Marketing Services Cost?

Paid email-marketing service providers base their rates on the number of email addresses in your mailing list. The average plan runs between $15 to $20 per month for up to 500 recipients with unlimited mailings within a given month. Compared to the cheapest bulk mail rates, email marketing is a bargain.

You can do even better with free email marketing services. I recommend Mail Chimp, Madmimi.com, ActiveCampaign.com and FineArtAmerica.com (FAA). Mail Chimp offers a free plan for up to 2,000 addresses with as many as 12,000 emails every month. FineArtAmerica.com is a free online marketing, print-on-demand and complete sales and order fulfillment resource for visual artists.

The FAA service is particularly helpful in promoting the work listed in your online gallery and on the free website that is also available for those who pay the nominal $30-per-year upgrade fee. With its easy-to-use formatting, it's a useful tool for showcasing your work on the FAA site.

Using Mail Chimp, in addition to FAA's email marketing services, gives you powerful additional features. These include list-building services such as opt-in forms, buttons and links.

You also can send auto-responder and drip campaigns, which are practical ways to send an automatic, single response or a series of timed responses to your subscribers. I'll discuss how and when to use these features later

Using email marketing services to drive traffic, create interest and make sales is a cost-effective and efficient way to promote your business and add new potential buyers to way to expand your business and your loyal fan base

Efficient Design for Email Marketing Is Essential

Understanding and using email marketing design techniques increase your readers' interest. Effective design will keep them reading your message.

Previously, I've talked about the importance of building your email-marketing list, and detailed options for different email-marketing services. Now I'll turn to email newsletter design.

Newsletter Design Tips

Start with a preheader. Email open rates differ. Naturally, you won't get every subscriber to open and read your email. Some will open it but not read the entire contents. A preheader, a strong secondary subject line, will enhance the open rate and click-through rate for your email marketing messages. It appears just after the subject line in an Inbox. For your readers, it briefly summarizes what the email is about before they open it. In effect, the preheader appears as the first line of copy above the body of your email.

It displays in some email programs, such as Gmail, Outlook and in most mobile email readers.

Use Headlines and Images

Use headlines with header tags, such as that provided by h2-level formatting, to break up blocks of text. Many readers are skimmers. You can give them the essence of what your email message contains by moving them through the copy with headlines. Keep your headlines short, informative and punchy.

If it makes visual sense, use a headline that relates to the second block of text, rather than the first. You won't lose readers by doing this. In some cases, the headline serves as a "teaser" that intrigues viewers to keep reading to discover the copy to which the headline relates.

Images

Understandably, in email marketing for artists, images are almost expected. They help tell your story visually. And they brighten your copy. Images help your reader more easily understand your email marketing message.

Always use the Alt-tag option on your images. ALT attribute text is the short line of copy that shows if a viewer hovers over the image. It also displays if your recipients' default is set not to display images in their browser.

Alt-tags are great selling tools in email marketing for artists. If you don't change the picture default name, an image might display as something like DSC-12115.jpg, which is annoying and useless. With image alt-tags, you add context and get a chance to tell your story more elaborately. Make your tag descriptive or a call to action, or both: "Get 25% off all images from the Waterfront Series until (expiration date).

Make your images the right size for your content. Don't use huge images directly from your camera or smartphone. Use Photoshop or some other photo-editing software to compress the image for web use. Check out Pixlr.com if you don't have Photoshop. It's a similar though slimmed-down online program.

Many of the images on this site I created using Canva.com. I heartily recommend it for its cost (free for many designs, or $1.00 per stock image) and ease of use. It offers standard templates for many social media and other frequently used shapes. Also, its Design School is an excellent way to learn how to make images look professional. Because graphic design requires different skill sets from fine art, Canva.com is a very useful resource for artists. It's been a blessing for me.

Content Blocks

Use short content blocks of only two to three short sentences each. This helps your design for the short attention span of most email readers. Using bullet points and numbered items is also useful in making your copy easier to read. They increase your results.

Call to Action and Links

Your email marketing newsletter is a sales and promotional tool. While it doesn't hurt to be friendly and sociable, that's not your goal. Make sure you have a call to action designated for your newsletter. Yours might be:

- announcing a special offer
- inviting readers to a show or exhibit
- giving them the opportunity to purchase direct from you
- inviting readers to a gallery opening
- asking them to take a survey

Your call to action can be a hyperlinked image or a text link, or both. Use text links to grab your readers' attention, or to direct them to something you're writing about. For instance, if you visited a local museum, provide the link to that museum in the copy. Or, if you have an image of artwork for sale on your website, link that to the order page.

Design Elements

Pay attention and you'll notice a greater use of white space in graphic design everywhere, including email marketing. You'll see how grocery flyers, for instance, are less crowded with items. Most fonts are eye-friendly, flat and without shadows, bevels and other Photoshop tricks. So make sure that you use simple, easy-to-read fonts too.

Use personalization sparingly and only where appropriate. Incorporating a person's name does make your copy friendlier, unless you overdo it. Then it becomes "sales-y" and a big turnoff. In most cases, just use the first name, or sometimes only a last name. People don't want to discover their addresses or phone numbers in your email marketing copy.

Navigation

If you have various sections or your copy is lengthy, then use the page navigation as part of your email marketing newsletter design. Navigation helps your readers quickly jump to the part they want to read. Anchor text is another way to help your readers navigate your newsletter. An example is to hyperlink a word or phrase that relates to the content where the link is pointing. This is preferable to using something generic, such as "Click Here."

These are the basics of successful email marketing newsletter design. Learn to incorporate them into your email marketing efforts and you'll begin to see growing interest in your newsletter. This will translate into more conversions to sales, in addition to better open rates and click rates for your newsletter.

In All Email Marketing, Content Is King

Email marketing for artists is a must for any comprehensive strategy designed to develop a successful art career. To be effective, your email marketing newsletters and messages need new, stimulating and relevant content. As with all successful endeavors, planning and focus are keys to success.

Organization & Planning = More Success & Less Stress

Email marketing for artists is the same as for any other business. When the deadline to start writing comes, having your content researched and ready is how to avoid stress and reduce the time it takes to compose your article. Rushing to find last-minute news and ideas for your content creates anxiety and wastes time and money.

Use a Content-Keeping System for Email Marketing

Evernote is the best way for clipping online content. It helps you quickly and easily capture and organize anything you find online. Microsoft One Note is also a convenient info-organization tool. You can copy any document from your computer to a "note," and you can copy and paste information from the internet into it. Keeping a physical folder with ideas for content is old school, but if maintaining a physical folder still works better for you, then do that — but at least be open to trying the digital alternative. You might surprise yourself.

Content Is King

The goal for your email marketing strategy is simple: Engage your subscribers with content that keeps them involved and excited. You want subscribers to anticipate your email newsletters and to enjoy the content.

It's About You, Just Not All About You

Use a mix of information about you and your art, including noteworthy news, which could be either personal or professional. Write about your current projects, events, sales and promotions, along with other enticing tidbits of useful, entertaining items of interest. Of course, your content needs to be about you. Nevertheless, the more you incorporate content not specific to you that both interests and intrigues your subscribers, the more your readers will be eager to receive and read your messages.

Here are 10 suggestions for producing innovative and relevant content:

1. Video content is compelling. If you're already creating short videos to help you stand out with your audience, put them in your newsletter. A great way of doing that is by inserting a tightly cropped screenshot image from the video. Then link the image to the streaming service, such as YouTube, where it's been uploaded. This avoids the problem of subscribers' email programs filtering embedded videos.

2. Special Deals. Provide exclusive invitations or offers only available to newsletter subscribers. Make it pay for them.

3. Ongoing Useful Content. Add a regular "Tips for Art Collectors" as a fun, ongoing component of your newsletter. A few suggestions include how to hang art, how to care for, place, frame or reframe, store and ship it; how to manage consignments; and how to use the secondary art market.

4. Guest posters. These will add a different perspective or expertise to keep your art marketing content stimulating. Guests could include other artists, a picture framer, a museum curator, another art collector or the organizer of the show where you exhibit.

5. Tap relevant news stories. Use news about you, your local art community or the whole art community to involve your readers. Ask for feedback. Set up alerts on Google Alerts for topics you believe would attract your readers. Include one for your name and business name to learn what others are saying about you.

6. Resources for ideas are abundant. Keep up on news, trends, events and opinions. *The New York Times* "Art & Design" and *Huffington Post* "Arts & Culture" pages are abundant resources for your email marketing story ideas.

7. Keep up with your competition. When it comes to email marketing for artists, it's necessary to know what other artists are doing. If you find something valuable, you can link to it, or write your own art

marketing content to add your opinion and perspective. If the other post's content is relevant to you, for instance funding arts in education, your follow-up post citing the original will extend the messages and keep the drumbeat and your addition going. Notify the original authors to let them know that you've linked to their copy. It might prompt a prized return link to your content.

8. Hang out in the same online spots as your buyers. Use these sources for research first and communication second. Follow your customers to find the groups and communities where they hang out. See what topics are trending within those groups. Perhaps there's a charity or activity that's caught everyone's attention, but you weren't aware of it or its relevance to your audience. Never be a phony, however. But if you're like-minded, feature your buyers' and their communities' interests in your art-marketing newsletter. Or contribute to their cause and recommend it in your newsletter.

9. Get personal. It's easy for some of us to share stories from our own lives. If that's not you, don't despair. Draw parallels from third-party examples. Those can include anything that inspires you. If you learned a valuable lesson from classic literature, for instance, perhaps something that deeply moved you from reading (or seeing, for that matter) *Les Miserables* or *Anna Karenina*, then tell that to your readers. Relate how your life, art or business has been affected by what you learned. Talk about how it informed or inspired your newest works. Sharing

at this level is compelling, especially when it includes your art and creative process.

10. Use keyword and trend tools. They help you get inside the thoughts of your best customers and prospects. Use the Google AdWords Keywords and the Wordtracker Free Keyword tools to build a list of how your customers search to find art and artists. Layer your research using the Google Trends tool. The point is, when you know what your collectors and prospects are looking and searching for, you can build your content around their interests. That's much more efficient than your guessing or publishing content based solely on your interests. Hopefully you'll find much common ground with your audience to build on. As with many points listed here, this discussion is intended primarily as an overview. Using keyword and trend tool research could be the subject of a lengthy post or e-book on its own.

A Wealth of Information from Search Engines

Doing your own research for your art marketing newsletter will result in a range of possibilities that you can incorporate to make your copy sparkle. Just as with making art, the more time you spend working with words, the more your copy expertise will grow.

You'll find a myriad of items you can include in your newsletter. Never forget that the primary purpose of email marketing for artists is to spur interest in you and your art, and to lead to sales. Make sure you have links to pages where your readers can find your art and buy it online.

Make a Schedule and Stick to It

Commit to sending your newsletter at least monthly. Anything less than that and your list will become stale, and your reader interest will wane. Those contacts are too valuable to lose.

10 Tips to Make Email Marketing More Effective

1. Use product pictures. Using multiple images gets more attention and more clicks. Product images can jump click rates by 50%.

2. Use short, engaging subject lines. Be precise, concise, and offer a benefit, if possible. You only have about two seconds to get a click and have your email opened.

3. Always post a link near the top. Make sure your link is above the fold. (Above the fold is a term from the newspaper industry that has carried over to internet marketing. It means having content on the first screen: before a reader has to scroll to see more.)

4. Make your links visible. Don't hide links in images or buttons. This is the opposite of call-to-action items on your website or blog where images improve click rates. If your reader's email program defaults to not showing images, there may be nothing for your user to click on.

5. Be specific. Tell readers to CLICK HERE TO SUBSCRIBE. You can decide on all caps or not, but don't

be shy about asking or telling your readers what you want them to do.

6. Repeat your call to action three times. Make a call-to-action "link sandwich" in your email newsletter. Ask once at the top, once again in the middle, and one last time at the bottom, or in the PS.

7. Avoid using "spam-y" words. "Free," "help," "percent off," "reminder" – these words, especially if repeated, can trigger spam filters and, in the process, cause your email provider to stop the delivery of your message. Your email provider should have a checking system for you to evaluate your copy for potential spam problems. Make sure you use it.

8. Vary your subject line. Running the same subject line will reduce your open rate. Use information that relates to the content in your body copy.

9. Include social sharing buttons. Including social sharing buttons will raise your click rate dramatically. Use at least three social sharing links, such as Facebook, Twitter and Instagram. This will give you much better click rate results than including only one social sharing link. Programs that display a smorgasbord of links can be confusing and ineffective.

10. Add a PS. Using a postscript has been a staple of top print copywriting techniques for decades. Adding a PS is a proven way to get more clicks on your email marketing for artists' campaigns. Make it relevant, mindful, and always include a call-to-action link.

Understanding How Readers Respond to Your Email

There's a difference between open rates and click rates in email marketing. Open rates are the percentage of your subscribers who actually open an email you've sent to them. Click rates are the percentage of readers who have opened your email, and who then click on a link in your email. This could be a link to an email sign-up form, such as CLICK HERE TO SUBSCRIBE. As an artist, having links to product pages on your website where a buyer can order something from you is a brilliant idea.

Every list has a portion of dead weight. These are subscribers who are not opening your email. They may have changed email addresses without informing you. They may have lost interest in reading your email. Or they may have experienced life changes that have caused them to ignore your messages.

Dead weight addresses hurt your deliverability rates with senders. Your email service provider and the large email services such as Gmail, Yahoo, Outlook, Go Daddy and others take note of your open rates. If your undelivered rate is high, you're more likely to have your email sent to a spam, junk or bulk folder.

You can segment this inactive part of your list and attempt to re-engage them. Use a compelling subject line and content to try and break through their inbox clutter. Check out excellent examples of re-engagement emails on the My Emma blog. The internet has a wealth of useful information on this and other email marketing topics. Try searching for "re-engagement email campaigns" as a starter.

Ultimately, as hard as it is to say goodbye, you should remove dead weight addresses from your list. They're not helping; in fact, they may be hurting your email marketing efforts. I know how you might feel. You worked hard to get those names on the list, so now you hate to let them go. But keep in mind it's not the size of the list that's the most important, it's secondary to the responsiveness of your subscribers that makes the difference in effectiveness and sales.

Before you jettison your non-responders wholesale, review your list to ensure there are no obvious names you don't want to let go. For those, you can pick up the phone, send a postcard and check your personal email contact list to be sure you have a more current address for them. Then move on.

Nevertheless, you never want to completely delete an address from your list. Instead, you want to suppress it. (Different providers use different nomenclature for this suppressed list.) This will save you time and grief if you move to a new email marketing service and you want to import those addresses that have unsubscribed or that you've removed. This will help you keep your new provider list fresh and prevent you from accidentally sending emails to people who have opted out of your list.

Maintaining your list to keep your deliverability rate high is important. You can write awesome emails with compelling content, but if they go to the spam folder, your efforts are in vain. Put it on your calendar now to review your unopened list quarterly. Find those addresses that haven't opened your email in the previous 90 days and re-engage them, or move them off your list. Create a series of emails designed to get their attention. Once you have your re-engagement series written, it will only take a short time to get this important task completed.

Building Your List

When it comes to marketing, it's easy to say that everything is important, but – besides crafting a consistent and impressive tone and style for your marketing – list-building is the key to your growth and profitability. How you go about it is every way you can imagine.

As explained earlier, you need to ask all the people you meet or contact for their permission before you add them to your list. Your contact manager database should have a field to indicate whether you have permission to email someone. If you don't, use direct mail to communicate with those whose permission you lack. Make sure you have a call to action when you send snail mail to get people to come to your site or blog and subscribe.

Just because people include their email addresses on their sites does not translate to an invitation to send them unsolicited email. This applies in particular to broadcast (all-subscriber) email. A single thoughtful message to someone regarding something other than a blatant solicitation to buy your art is acceptable as standard business correspondence. However, it's not a license to build a form letter and robotically insert names in fields to give the impression of personal communication.

Here Are Ways to Build Your List:

- Ensure your email opt-in is prominent on your home page and other relevant pages of your website and your blog.
- Offer something for free. You might recall how Hazel Dooney and Banksy both give free, high-quality digital downloads. It could be a three-pack of note cards, a mini print or a report you've done on some art topic, which will get you a snail mail or email address.
- Start a blog with content that will build traffic over time. Have your email newsletter sign-up visible and easy to use.
- Create a publicity campaign about your newsletter, your most recent work or your charitable activity.
- Comment on another artist's blog or site.
- Write and submit articles for *Huffington Post*, *Forbes* and other national online publishers.
- Join and participate in art-related or culture-related forums. (This is not to be confused with art business forums where you find other artists who are your best prospects for encouragement, but not for sales.)
- Write about artists you admire or about art history or some other aspect of art that will drive traffic to your blog or website.

- Ask your subscribers to share your newsletter, and then give them a link to tweet or add to their Facebook page.
- Run contests that require entering an email address to participate.

Use Proper Email Etiquette on Initial Follow-ups

Start with reminding your recipients where they met you. Was it at an event, a show or social gathering? Did they inquire about something specific? Do you have common acquaintances? Have they commented on your blog? Include something in the subject line that jogs their memory, for example "Met You at the Scottsdale Art Walk."

Don't delay your follow-up. The sooner you send your email, the more likely your prospects are to remember you and open it. Most people set up their email to put addresses they open on their accepted list. Using an inviting subject line helps get your mail open. Avoid words or phrases that trigger anti-spam filters. You can search for "spam filter words" to find them. This will keep your email from going into the spam or junk mail folder.

Choose a Reliable Email-Services Provider

You won't be able to manage a subscriber list using Outlook or some other email desktop client. It's likely that your internet service provider (ISP) or email provider will have limits on the number of emails you can send in a day.

Use your favorite search engine to query for "email service provider reviews" to find a suitable, reliable service. My current favorite is Madmimi.com. You can create an account there and start with a free option. For 500 names, the current cost is $10 per month; 10,000, for $42.

Another option is ActiveCampaign.com. It's more robust than Madmimi as it offers marketing automation, which I will discuss later. For those new to email marketing, I suggest Madmimi because of its ease of use and superb customer service. Other services worth considering are MailChimp (not my favorite due to its complexity of use), GetDrip.com and Convertkit.com.

Marketing automation is a combination of software and marketing tactics that allows marketers to send personalized content to specific audience segments. Rather than one size fits all, marketing automation is a system to nurture prospects in a process that helps move them from strangers to happy customers. It typically produces more customer engagement that leads to more sales and higher profits. As mentioned above, I have more to tell you about this system later in this book.

Your provider will email creation tools to build templates for newsletters, surveys and more. Get a list of what's available to find the best ones for your needs. Your provider will have free tutorials, site tours and description of the site's features.

Some email programs have an autoresponder feature. This allows you to send a series of emails on a timeline of your choice. Using a feature like this is an excellent way to add value to your service (and thus your sales) and encourage subscribers to join. An autoresponder series is synonymously known as a drip campaign, "dripping" content to your readers on an ongoing basis. Drip campaigns are discussed in detail later.

Your topic will be the key to your success. Whether you're talking about art history, local lore, seasonal offerings, recipes or poems doesn't matter as much your passion and the fact that the topic has relevance to your readers.

Here again is a place where you might hire a copywriter to help you create a knockout series of drip emails. Look for one who also has SEO experience and consider having that writer work on your website content as well.

Tips on Newsletter Mailings

- As mentioned with individual emails, your subject line is critical. It should be keyword- and benefit-driven.
- Add value. Give your readers a reason to open and read your email. For example, offer tips for hanging or displaying art, discounts on purchases or shipping, partner discounts, and more.
- Ask questions. Include polls or surveys to help learn what's relevant to your readers.
- Consider adding video. Many email provider services offer this option.

- Educate and entertain. Reciting dry facts about you or your art won't work, but providing insights and anecdotes will.
- Don't keep emailing to recipients who never open your emails. Consider a unique direct mail campaign to re-engage them or, ultimately, weed them off your list.
- Think about segmenting your list demographically or geographically.

Anything you can do to make your mailing more targeted to your audience will make it more efficient.

Publishing an electronic newsletter is a great use for email marketing. It can incorporate announcements about everything you're doing, so include any new pieces in the works or those that have just been made available, as well as any scheduled appearances or openings, or upcoming shows where you'll be exhibiting.

You can make your newsletter a source of information that goes beyond what's happening with you. Use it to reprint, with permission, articles of interest to your readers. For example, if you paint in an abstract style, educate your readers about the history of the style. If your market is local or regional, talk about museums, fairs, gatherings and other culture-related topics.

If you're a gourmand, gourmet, a great chef or a wine connoisseur, then use that knowledge to write entertaining articles about those subjects. The point is to make your newsletter something your subscribers will want to open and read. If you provide details that are not all self-serving and aimed directly at making art sales, you'll make yourself and your art that much more appealing.

Ask your readers to forward your newsletter to their family and friends. Have an email sign-up prominent on the first and every other appropriate page. You can use a mix of text links and HTML sign-up box scripts to vary the offer.

Email Marketing Bonus Content

Thoughts from other art marketing experts can be productive as well. Here's an excellent example of tapping additional resources to expand one's thinking on a topic. Use the link to a podcast with Jason Horejs, owner of Xanadu Gallery and publisher of RedDotBlog.com, and me. We talk and give advice for about 60 minutes [http://artmarketing-news.com/art-2-market-sessions] And then scroll to the bottom of the page to find this video. There are many others there that you'll also find informative and helpful.

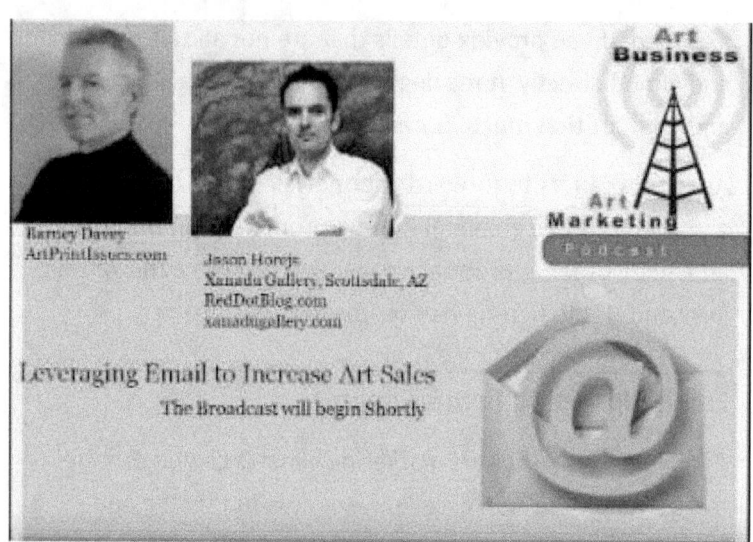

I can't stress the importance of email marketing enough. There is no more powerful tool available for you. Make list building a high priority, and then send to your list regularly. Do these things first. Don't put them off to work on secondary tasks. As the late Stephen Covey said, "Keep the main thing the main thing."

CHAPTER 7

Marketing Automation

Marketing today is less about the sale and more about the journey. –John Jantsch

Marketing Automation for Artists

The methods of finding prospects and developing them into customers are evolving, particularly in the digital age. Changes that might have taken decades not that long ago happen now in years and months.

The internet has substantially changed everything in communications, commerce, entertainment and more. The companies that are doing the best and growing their brands and sales in this new environment are adopting, adapting and reacting to what feels like constant flux.

Despite how the internet creates change, some things never change. An appropriate example here is the KNOW – LIKE – TRUST continuum. People's buying habits are the same online as offline. The tendency is for them to go through that continuum before making a purchase. They ask themselves, "If I don't know you, how can I like or trust you?" Consumers are educated and have their guard up when dealing with new potential vendors. It's why services such as Yelp and Angie's List are so popular. When they don't know you, they seek validation.

There is no Yelp for artists. Buyers are on their own. With that understanding, you can use this information to treat your customers to a pleasant experience. They might like your art right away. But to make a sale, you need to earn their trust and for that to happen, they need to develop a sense of familiarity with you. That's how you'll sell more art over the course of your career.

Visual artists have mostly been on the sidelines of the rapid changes regarding marketing. I see more using new technology, moving into digital art making, digital printing and even some into 3D printing. Artists with vision will harness these advantages and change art in unimaginable ways. But in marketing their art virtually, all of them are stymied by using techniques from decades ago.

The marketing front has changed, too. It used to be a that a marketing "plan" consisted of creating a product, then driving cold traffic (prospective buyers) to a landing or sales page that converts visitors' interest into sales (product + landing page traffic = sales).

That methodology lasted for years. It evolved from basic, almost a brute force kind of marketing into a more sophisticated approach with softer pitches, better bonuses and tighter control on the demographics being sent to a landing page.

This scenario worked very well at first in many industries and made lots of internet marketers wealthy in the process. Eventually, this online model became "oversold" and stopped working. The buying public had become smarter and less patient with what they came to regard as such in-your-face advertising. In fact, today we mostly ignore those efforts.

A new way of doing things grew out of frustration with the low return on investment (ROI) from doing things the old-fashioned way. The new method takes more time, offers more value and works more closely to mimic human behavior than past marketing models. In effect, it breeds a familiarity that helps make sales.

Instead of sending cold traffic to sales pages, smart digital marketers use a multistep process. Not unlike dating. There's a range of approaches that work. You know it's ineffective or even offensive for a guy in a club or nightspot to approach a girl he's never met and ask for a kiss. It's equally unproductive and inappropriate to ask a prospect new to your art and to you to buy your work on the very first "speed date," your first contact or communication.

A real potential connection happens only after a meaningful relationship has been forged. You get to know the person.

Who they are. What they do. Where they live. How they feel about things important to you. It's a natural progression of peeling away layers to get to a place of "know, like and trust."

Without "know, like and trust," the "kiss" connection just isn't going to happen. The same applies to selling art. If your goal is to sell to buyers directly (something I strongly recommend), your success hinges on building a mutual knowledge of one another (know), a solid connection (like) and trust.

This is where artists get jammed. They're still trying to sell too fast. They're not using methods that help them build rapport and trust with potential patrons. I don't blame them. No one has been there to help them understand this sales paradigm shift or guide them to think about doing things differently – at least until now.

The previous section on using drip campaigns goes a long way toward helping artists improve their marketing. But they shouldn't and don't need to stop there because there's so much more they can do to move up to modern marketing techniques.

I'm not going to discuss how to get traffic. I assume you're already doing something to raise awareness of your art and your brand – you! It could be Facebook posts and ads. Or hanging out in forums on LinkedIn. You might be attending meetings of associations and groups that you think might attract prospects for your art. There are dozens of ways to lure traffic to your site. That's not the problem.

Where artists are falling down is in not having a plan for what happens after someone shows up at their site. Many are getting better about having some sort of opt-in form on their blogs and websites. Unfortunately, those opt-in forms are widely ineffective today since most of us have developed banner blindness and can easily ignore requests for our email addresses.

Even when we do encounter a web form, we ignore it anyway because there's no quid pro quo for our information. People aren't sufficiently motivated to divulge their email addresses just because you promise to send them more email. Everyone I know already gets too much and most of us don't want more. So, without the proper incentive, a web form request for an email address is, with rare exceptions, pointless.

What's an Artist to Do?

Because there's no easy answer, most artists get stuck right here. They have a hard time getting opt-ins to their email list. And when they do get an email, they start asking too quickly for sales, or they have no follow-up plan beyond that initial prospective buyer contact. In most cases, the level of outbound communication falls far below the degree of sophistication of the prospect.

Before I talk about what artists should do, let me describe the process savvy marketers in other fields are using to move customers along a path to a sale. As I said before, it's a multistep process that takes time to complete and there is a precise, thoughtful formula for what goes into each step. Moreover, the process contains testing all along the way to refine what's working and to kick to the curb anything that isn't.

The current preferred method of turning cold traffic into hot sales has five parts:

1. Valuable Content
2. Lead Magnet
3. Tripwire
4. Core Offer
5. Profit Maximizer

Valuable Content

If you want people's attention, you need to have content that appeals to them in some way. The best content either scratches an itch or relieves a pain. These are not exclusive. You can create compelling content that's just so fascinating that it's hard to resist. It's possible, but hard to do consistently.

An example of scratching an itch might be an article on how to do something that interests the prospect. For a wannabe artist, for instance, it might be deconstructing how a famous painting was created. It might be explaining something in layman's terms about art creation. Or something in the art field that you take for granted but nonetheless that might seem mysterious to art buyers. It could be as simple as a drawing lesson. You get the idea, I'm sure.

An example of relieving a pain might be how to restore an old keepsake photograph. It could be how to care for a vintage poster or clean and care for an aging original. It might be an explanation of how the secondary art market works or how to safely buy art online. Perhaps it's just a trick on how to correctly and squarely hang multiple pieces.

You know your audience and avatar, especially if you've taken my How to Find Collectors training. The first lesson goes far into helping you get to know more about your customers and potential buyers than you can imagine. The insights you gain from this exercise are powerful. They will help you make intelligent decisions about everything you do regarding marketing your art. You can use your avatar insights to think deeply about collectors' itches and pains and then can create content to touch on those points.

If creating content isn't your thing, there are freelancers eager to help you with it. If you balk at the idea of hiring a freelancer, or creating your own content because of the time and money it takes, you need an attitude adjustment.

That's because it's the opposite of what you think. The reality is you cannot afford not to find a way to communicate with your patrons, buyers and prospects on a higher level. You risk losing sales and relationships and miss opportunities to make new relationships and build your business.

Of course, if you continue to balk at change, it might be time to evaluate what you want from your career, and what you're actually willing to invest and to do to make it successful. There's no shame in deciding that not pursuing a full-time career as an artist is your best path. Being a businessperson isn't the right fit for lots of otherwise talented, smart artists.

On the other hand, if it's your burning passion to become a successful, full-time artist, then it's time to invest in the business side of your career and get your marketing up to speed for the future. Some things will never change: for instance, that if you show your art on a steady basis to enough qualified buyers, you'll sell your work. In the past, the way to get sales was through galleries and other third-parties such as publishers, licensing agents and so forth.

What's advantageous today is that buyers are more ready and willing to buy directly from artists. However, artists can only succeed at making this happen if they use the tools and techniques at their disposal in ways that resonate with buyers. If you are going to sell them, you have to romance them.

The steps laid out here work. They follow the path of starting small and working your way up to a place where you have established a "know, like and trust" relationship with your prospective buyers. Nothing happens overnight.

When you get busy and stay busy working on building business relationships and friendships, you will soon enough reap a cumulative, exponential harvest. The tipping point is inevitable: you'll start seeing more sales and new patterns of sales, and you'll know they happened because you set

goals, took deliberate actions, tested and refined your results, and stayed optimistic and aggressive in your marketing.

Lead Magnet

So, let's say your skillful promotion for the valuable quid
pro quo content you offer gets you an email address. Or, if
you're using Facebook advertising, it gets you a retargeting
pixel. You'll either send an email with an offer for your lead
magnet, that incentive you use to tempt readers to connect
with you further, or start a Facebook retargeting campaign
that offers your lead magnet. Think of it as a SMOT (second
moment of truth, per marketing), following the FMOT (first
moment of truth), the opening page itself.

You can suggest your lead magnet within your initial valuable content as an option. This works best when you know
your audience well or if there's a good chance they might
know you, if even slightly.

A lead magnet is something of value you're giving away.
The best are things easily understood, highly desirable and
quickly consumed. It's usually in the form of a digital download. You may recall the mention of Hazel Dooney offering
hi-res images that are small, but suitable for framing. That's
a perfect example of a lead magnet.

Infographics, checklists and post compilations also make
great lead magnets. Short books, reports and how-tos work
well, too. Sometimes expanding on your valuable content

or aggregating some of it makes an appropriate lead magnet. Getting multiple uses of your content like that, repurposing it, is a smart, efficient and acceptable way to extend the investment you made in creating your content in the first place.

What's happened with placing a lead magnet is that, with new clients, you've begun a relationship by establishing yourself as an authority on a topic that interests them. By asking for and getting their email address, you've now received in return a micro-commitment from them. They have entrusted you with their email address. That's good – for both of you.

Tripwire Offer

You can always add a tripwire as well. That's something of greater value than a lead magnet and usually a product or service sold on your website for a higher price. When you see an author offering a book for free, plus a $6.99 shipping fee, you're encountering a tripwire. You can bet a core offer, the full-priced retail product, is waiting in the wings. As is the upsell to the profit maximizer offer, which defines itself.

Your customer path is a series of mutual commitments in an ongoing relationship. It begins with the tripwire offer – the micro-commitment – that shows interest from the buyers who have moved beyond providing an email address to trusting you with their credit card information. It's a real-time development of your nurturing the relationship you've developed with them. It's the digital equivalent of making friends, each of you checking to see how the friendship is evolving.

A tripwire is an offer of great value at a bargain price. Your offer. By this time in the communication process, it also involves tripwire purchasers self-selecting and segmenting themselves as potential buyers. You don't give your email address and then your credit card information unless you like what's being offered. By the tripwire stage, you've achieved the first full level of the "know, like and trust" continuum.

Some tripwire suggestions for artists are notecards, mini prints, posters, portfolios, sketches, books or anything else you can think of that has value to your target audience. It should be something that your prospects find of interest and value, and that they know you'd otherwise be selling for a higher price on your website. Experimenting with different offers and different price points is the only way to figure out the ideal offer.

Core Offer

For most artists, this is going to be original artwork, perhaps a limited edition or a higher-priced, open-edition print. There is timing involved in how quickly you roll out your offers. While your lead magnet and tripwire can come right on top of each other, the core offer takes more strategy. You may want to take some time before you make your pitch.

As always, testing is the only way to get the timing right. Your audience, your art and your price points can affect how long you wait after you make a tripwire sale before you make your core offer. You could extend your core offer with a thank-you email from the tripwire deal. In fact, that's a good place to start. See how it works. But give it enough time and repetitions before you decide to make any changes about core offer timing.

You can set up an automated responder or drip campaign to send your core offer to your prospects. Try posting something weekly for five or six weeks, then drop to every other week for a couple of months. If your potential buyers are still on the fence and haven't shown any interest in a particular piece of art, consider a follow-up phone call. In addition to a personal and possible sales contact, this gives you a chance to find out how your marketing is working – or not.

The feedback from the phone call can help you refine your sales methods. Knowing why customers aren't buying is invaluable. Instead of guessing and testing, you can address objections and head off problems before they arise. When you've exhausted all your options for getting an immediate sale from the call, be sure to keep each phone contact in your general broadcast list. If you have multiple lead magnets, they may again segment themselves for input into another marketing funnel for a different lead magnet.

A Further Word about Emails

Your most important email is your welcome email. Some of this is detailed in a previous section on drip campaigns. I include additional information here since it's specific to the current topic of marketing automation. At the moment your new prospects opt into your list for the first time, they're most receptive. Make sure you introduce yourself and provide insights into your business. Take the time to explain how often and what you send by email. Give brief instructions on how to whitelist your email address to ensure it makes it to their inbox.

Your initial email should include links to previous posts so readers get an idea of how you create and provide content. If all that information is lengthy, you might want to break it up into two separate emails to keep from writing a novel on your first welcome email. If you're set up to send emails for a lead magnet or tripwire, you want to be aware of when you've scheduled those to go out so you don't overwhelm recipients with too much email.

You should segment your list so you keep those prospects who are moving through your funnel from getting your broadcast emails until you think the prospects are ready to receive them. You want to keep them focused on what's important and relevant to your marketing at the moment. Again, it's really a matter of avoiding TMI (too much information). Besides, you certainly don't want to confuse them by dropping another lead magnet in their inbox too soon.

That can throw off the current targeted marketing sequence to which they've already responded.

Profit Maximizer

Imagine you've just landed a core offer sale. Congratulations! Keep that up and your income will become predictable, and your future more secure. A profit maximizer is an upsell to something of greater value than a core offer.

As with the tripwire thank-you email, you can provide a profit maximizer offer in your core offer thank-you email. An example of a profit maximizer is a suite of images or artworks. Perhaps one large and two smaller complementary pieces. Or one original and two prints. It might even be to offer one of your masterpieces, bigger and more elaborate than your standard originals.

You might use a profit maximizer to tender an offer to do a commission. Or you could have a club or society where you charge an annual or monthly fee with certain products included and substantial discounts on others, or free shipping, or whatever makes sense to you that works. It's a great place to stretch your imagination. Use the brainstorming exercise of writing down 100 items that you would never use for a profit maximizer. I'm confident you'll come up with a splendid idea you wouldn't have thought of without the brainstorming.

With profit maximizers, it's always going to come down to how well you know your audience. Use your creativity to brainstorm for unique ideas for products or services to fill each of the five steps in your marketing process for this offer. If it seems by this point that the complete process from initial contact through profit maximizer has become too complicated, or if you conclude this last step doesn't fit your business model, you may decide to forgo it. Maybe you've determined that your particular market segment just won't respond to it. That's your call, as always.

The reason for taking on any sophisticated marketing is always the same. You're looking to take prospects the end of the AIDA (Attention – Interest – Desire = Action) continuum. You value your work. You want to see it sold and out in the world, ready to be handed down as an heirloom through generations. What you're learning by reading this post is the best recipe for cooking up long-term success just like that for your career.

None of these actions are set in stone. They're strongly suggested, however, because they've been battle-tested in many different vertical markets. The process works. To be sure, trying something like this will shake up your marketing and breathe new life into it.

If you feel you're stuck or just marking time by using antiquated and ineffective marketing techniques, then by all means give this strategy a try. You've nothing to lose and everything to gain by pushing yourself to try new things, in this case the new marketing technology and techniques for a new age.

CHAPTER 8

Blogging

The influence of blogging is overall a very positive force in the media. – Garrett Graff

Blogging for Artists

Blogs (short for weblog) began as web-based journals or diaries. As a blog author, you're known as a "blogger": someone who regularly publishes content on a certain topic or range of subjects. As a blogger, you want to be known for something. You should be able to describe the mission of your blog in one or two sentences.

By adding frequent and regular postings, you'll begin to create a virtual blog community. That community is comprised of like-minded folks interested in the topics you write about. When you allow your blog visitors to post feedback to your journal entries, they become even more committed to the community and therefore to your site. This interaction makes a connection and can strengthen your relationships with your collectors and potential buyers – which you can leverage into greater sales.

With regard to art marketing and developing an online presence, I consider having a personal blog to be a primary tool in the hierarchy of what's most important. From my perspective, a blog ranks only behind a good domain name and a personal website.

In the past, I recommended using an RSS feed to help distribute your blog. I no longer make that suggestion due to the RSS blogger's not having control of the subscriber list. I can sign up for your blog and become an avid fan using an RSS feed. But you'll never know who I am or how to contact me. That means your only way of communicating with me is via RSS feed. You can't send an email to a segment of your list and reach me with it. As I've already stressed, getting email opt-ins is a high-value proposition for you, and RSS feeds deny you the opportunity.

A blog is more interactive – more like a conversation – while a newsletter is more formal. And, although the lines between these two terms and venues have blurred as they've developed, it may be helpful to think of a blog more as a journal. An online diary of your personal experience as an artist. There's a place in your marketing for both. As much as anything, it's ultimately a matter of personal preference. You can do both, or one or the other. You might start with blogging and then see if you also have the capacity for a newsletter.

Your readers can interact with your blog topic in the form of comments. Some blogs – either by design or because of the content – are more suitable for reader comments and interaction. You'll gain a feel for how you want to work this as you develop your own blogging style.

I've written numerous posts on Art Marketing News about blogging for artists. Some are included in this book.

If you wonder why artists should blog, I have the answer for you: It's the best way to grow an email list and communicate on a regular basis with your buyers and prospects.

Some Reasons Why Artists Should Blog

- help you sell your art direct to buyers
- promote awareness and gain interest in your art
- grow your email list
- control your digital brand and reputation
- drive traffic to your website
- open the door to guest blogging
- create links and SEO value for traffic and search engine rankings
- make a positive influence on juried show judges
- introduce your work to gallery owners
- provide content for social media platforms
- sell without the middleman

I believe artists need to build a relationship with art collectors who buy from them with no intermediary. The more art buyers you have that know you, the less likely you are to take a hit when one of your distribution channels fail.

It's only a matter of time before a gallery will close, or your favorite social media site pulls the rug from under you. You have zero control of these distribution channels. Their customers are not your customers. Anything you do to make sales through third parties such as galleries and social media is an expense causing you to earn less money.

Don't get me wrong; galleries make a difference. I believe in using galleries. I also know social media can help you sell art. I just think these less secure options need to be regarded in the right perspective. That is, as secondary or tertiary methods of selling your art.

Selling art to buyers one-on-one is your primary way to stay profitable and in control. If selling directly to collectors is not your first method of getting your art to market, start to fix that now. It's your future. No one cares more about your career than you do. Relationships with direct buying customers give you control. They form a solid foundation that minimizes inevitable problems from third-party sales networks.

Does Selling Direct to Buyers Appeal to You?

If you agree that building a collector base is a solid strategic goal, then you should understand why I believe you need to blog. It's one thing to recognize that marketing to buyers and creating a collector base are good things. It's another to get the job done.

Artists should blog because it's the most efficient way to build an email list and communicate with buyers and prospects. To sell anything, you need interest from many potential buyers. It's a numbers game.

The bigger your pool of prospects, the more you will sell.

On average, 4-10% of your interested prospects and current customers may buy from you in a given year. Many factors affect the range. You might have done an extraordinary show, or produced an exciting series of art that takes wing and sells as fast as you make it. You may have improved your communications and kept your prospects enthralled with your art.

You can only do so many "extra" shows. And, we all know shows are never a given thing. You can do your best and still not have a stellar outcome at a show. You always strive to make art that will jump off the walls, but experience tells you that sometimes you strike gold in a way that's not easy to replicate.

You don't always know why certain images create extraordinary interest. It's a random dynamic that's part of creating art. It's the same for authors, filmmakers, playwrights and all creatives. Be grateful when it happens and work it to your benefit as you can.

More Thoughts on Why Artists Should Blog

Yes, you can do all sorts of things to create interest in your work. But to build sustained interest from direct buying collectors, you need a list. There is no other option. Period. Without a list of interested prospects, you have nothing.

A blog can entertain, inform, educate, delight and keep readers involved.

A successful blog sustains interest in your work. It helps you grow your email list and sell your art. Your prospects may love you and love your artwork. That doesn't mean they're willing to give you permission to email them without a reason. Besides, they won't give out their email address with the express purpose of your sending sales messages to them. It doesn't work that way.

As I noted above, only a small percentage of potential buyers purchase something within a 12-month time span. You need to engage the rest on a regular basis to keep their interest. A blog does that for you. If all you do is send occasional emails that are notices to come to a show, or that you have new artwork to sell, your list will wither and die.

With email lists, there is no status quo. If your list isn't growing and getting better, it's getting worse. It takes active participation from you to develop and to maintain your email marketing list. It won't grow and it won't be effective for you unless you manage it with care.

A viable, responsive email list is a crucial part of your business. It's a bottom-line asset that will make the difference between success and failure for most artists. Nothing will help you grow and maintain your email list better than a blog.

Your blog is your best communication tool.

Your blog gives you a valid, efficient method to request email addresses from prospects. It also gives you permission to send a frequent communication to them. So it keeps awareness for you and your art high.

You can use your blog posts as content for your social media. Images from your posts can go on Pinterest and Instagram. You can publish links to your posts on your Facebook page and in your LinkedIn account.

Your Blog Is a Multipurpose Tool

It is the dynamic marketing complement for your website, which is static by comparison. You can repurpose your blog posts to publish a group of them as an e-book or even a physical book. You can use your blog posts to show as examples to support your requests to guest blog on a top blog in your market.

Your website is your virtual real estate on the internet. You have exclusive rights to that virtual space. No one can take it away, change the rules, or stop traffic from coming or buyers from buying.

Your blog is a phenomenal brand management tool. You have a brand, which is your reputation. Before the days of the internet, a personal brand came from what galleries and the media said about you. To a much lesser extent, what word of mouth said about you and your art. Today, everyone knows everything about everybody.

A blog puts you in control of your digital brand and your reputation. If you post to your blog with frequency, then when others search your name, they'll find your posts, and your website as a result. If you don't blog on a frequent basis, what searchers will find is what others have to say about you. Who wants that when you have the option to control your brand?

Search Engines and Blogs

Search engines love blogs because they're dynamic. Your website and newsletter, on the other hand, are static. You publish the information and it stays as is – indefinitely. Blogs are a continual source of new, fresh information. If you establish a blog and begin to write consistently and authoritatively on topics of interest to you and your readers, you'll start to find your blog gaining high page-rank value on Google. You'll also find it ranking high for the keywords and keyword phrases relevant to your art business.

Search engines are about one thing: relevance. The goal of a search engine is to provide results most relevant to any single query it receives. In a perfect world, if you enter a query, you should find the source or answer you seek in the top five results. In most cases, search engines consider newer information to be more relevant than older information. In addition to the many other positive marketing aspects you derive from using a blog, the improved SEO results alone should encourage you to begin one right away.

Nevertheless, although I emphasize the value of email marketing, it's not as effective as it once was due to spam and junk mail filters, general inbox overload and fears of viruses. Blogs help fill the void left by the downturn in email marketing. They offer a means to communicate with your reader base of collectors, prospects, artist friends and industry-related contacts.

Blogging helps support your email marketing efforts by enabling subscription options that allow your visitors to be notified each time you update your blog. Since your blog entries are archived on your blogging software site, they can be retrieved and searched by your visitors at any time. This is in contrast to your newsletters, which are typically deleted soon after being read.

Blog Essentials

To begin, you need to decide on these four things:

- blogging software/platform
- blog title
- blog theme
- content

A blog is a website specially configured to allow you to easily maintain all the functions of efficiently managing your blogging activities. While there are both free and paid services you can choose from to use for your blog platform, I recommend avoiding the free sites.

Here's why:

- The free site is on a subdomain of the provider, for example, worldfamousartist.blogspot.com.
- You have less control of your settings.
- You must abide by terms of services for the provider.
- Blogs may be deleted without notice if they become identified as spam.
- Blogs may be deleted if your site is hacked.
- Custom design and the range of templates available are limited.

But the main reason to pay for your own blog hosting is that *you* own the domain, and that personal ownership is something I stressed earlier. When you use a free service, *it* owns the domain. That means your blog isn't portable. You can't go into the control panel and forward your blog and all its content to another provider.

That's because each post you write will have a unique URL for it. And so, should you want to move your content, since you neither own or control the BlogSpot.com domain name, you can't redirect readers from it to your new site.

As a result, you wind up potentially losing all the links created over the years to your archived posts. This means that links from both search engines and those created by your readers to your blog will no longer work.

Suppose, for example, you're on BlogSpot. The URL for your blog posts would be something like barneydaveyart.blogspot.com. When you decide to leave BlogSpot, all the links to all the posts on BlogSpot cannot be redirected to your new site because you neither own nor control the Blogspot.com domain. You can export your posts, but all the links to them stay pointing to BlogSpot – where your readers won't find you anymore. You can keep your BlogSpot blog live, but then you'd have duplicate content if you imported your old posts into the new blog platform. Can you see why this is such a potential nightmare? Besides, having your own domain looks more professional.

Here's an excerpt from Fusion.net:

> Artist Dennis Cooper has a big problem on his hands: Most of his artwork from the past 14 years just disappeared.
>
> It's gone because it was kept entirely on his blog, which the experimental author and artist has maintained on the Google-owned platform Blogger since 2002 (Google bought the service in 2003). At the end of June, Cooper says he discovered he could no longer access his Blogger account and that his blog had been taken offline.

There's more to the story. Cooper's art was for mature audiences. He may have violated Google's terms of service (TOS) with it. Why it took 14 years for Google to act is unknown, as is why it also shut down his Gmail account. The bottom line is that you can be deemed in violation of TOS from any provider and consequently have your content removed. Legal remedy is expensive and comes with no guarantees. Backups that you own and control are essential.

Naming Your Blog

When it comes to a blog title, if possible, you should make it a subdomain of your website, such as blog.yourdomain-name.com. It might be tempting to purchase a cool domain name to use, but then you're watering down your primary website domain, your brand, in the process. You'll also be required to market two unique domain names, which is a lot of effort for little (no) gain.

If you've already started down the path of a single domain for your website and your blog, you have to weigh whether to stick with your decision or not. That will depend on how long your blog has been published, how many posts it contains, what your blog Google page rank is and how difficult it will be to make the change. In many cases, you 're better served by sticking with the two domain names rather than going through the trouble to change.

Initially, I built my Art Marketing News blog using Typepad. It's a paid service that, overall, offers users many valuable options. Still, while Typepad does allow me to do domain mapping so that I can mask my actual Typepad blog URL – barneydavey.blogs.com, from an SEO perspective, it's still far from ideal. What's more, I was stuck using the themes it provides, which – while numerous – are more limited than I'd like. If I were beginning a blog today or making a recommendation for a new blogger, I'd use WordPress on a paid self-hosting site.

A theme gives your blog its unique look. No matter how you choose to publish your blog, you'll have options for selecting a corresponding theme. Those choices will include color, type and graphics. Additionally, you'll be able to choose from one, two or three columns within a theme. I recommend keeping your sidebar columns on the right so your main content will load first. Using a single sidebar column also minimizes clutter and distraction, making it a better choice than a busier, three-column format.

If you take my suggestion and go with a self-hosted version of WordPress, then you'll need a theme. There are both free and paid theme options available. Naturally, you'll find more customization with the premium themes, and likely more features as well. There are too many possibilities to discuss them in-depth here – and new ones are added all the time. I use a theme from StudioPress.com. Page-builder themes, such as Divi and ThriveThemes, are popular these days. Ask around and do your research to get comfortable with your choice. There are also page-builder plugins such as Beaver Builder and Visual Composer. Take the time to research your options before moving forward. You'll be glad you did.

Content Is the Key

As with email marketing, and all communications for that matter, the quality of your content is essential to making your investment in creating it pay off.

When it comes to what to write, you'll find that no rules apply. However, as in so many social situations, while you're free to discuss any topic you choose, that doesn't mean you should. I'd avoid controversial subjects since your mission is to promote your art career and find readers who'll buy your art. Getting entangled in politics, religion or even about "rights" content is going to be a distracting sideshow.

As for topics, a piece I wrote in an Art Marketing News post titled "A Year of Blog Topics for Artists – No Reason to Hold Back Now" will prove helpful. It offers useful ideas on blog topics you can use to get started. If you're committed to your blog, you'll find that a side benefit of having the discipline to write regularly will be the blossoming of your blog voice. Just as you paint with a certain flair or style, your blog posts will speak with a unique voice. As you develop your style, you'll find topics are everywhere.

Things to Remember as You Write Your Posts

- Make them creative and exciting. You want to touch your readers with your sincerity and passion about your creative process.
- Include keywords and keyword phrases in your blog post title and in your content. Being consistent with

both will help you get top rankings with search engines.

- Post frequently. Twice a week or more is great, or once a week at a minimum. Doing so will bring you more return visitors, increase your blog subscriptions and garner more comments from site visitors.
- Don't rely strictly on a spell checker. You need to proofread your entries or have someone else do it for you. If your writing skills are weak, or your English is poor, consider using a service such as www.gramlee.com to get professional help. There's no shame in doing that, but there is in publishing shoddy and poorly written blog posts.
- I use Grammarly.com and the Hemingwayapp.com to help me write better copy.
- If you have the budget, you can find companies that specialize in creating social media content for you. They'll ghostwrite blog posts and items for your Twitter and Facebook accounts as well. That said, I have a difficult time seeing how this would work for artists whose content is far more personal than, for instance, that of some corporation.

Follow Other Bloggers and Art Bloggers

How much have you learned about making art by observing what the best artists do to create their work? Well, the same goes for learning how to be a better blogger. Start following artists who have a good following and who use blogging effectively.

Here are some resources to help you:

- [49 Creative Geniuses Who Use Blogging to Promote Their Art](#) from SmartBlogger.com
- [Top 50 Art Blogs to Follow](#) from VisualNews.com
- [Top 10 Art Blogs to Follow](#) from ArtBusiness-News.com, including my ArtMarketingNews.com in the #1 spot
- [13 Art Blogs to Follow](#) from TheArtLeague.org

Promoting Your Blog

Once you've published your blog, you'll need to promote it. I suggest you get about 6-10 posts under your belt before you put too much effort into your promotion. It's so easy to start a blog, but even easier to quit one. As a result, abandoned blogs litter the webscape. That's the reason why I, as a longtime blogger, am not inclined to promote any new bloggers until I see they've established some continuity and staying power.

When ready, you should publicize your blog everywhere you can, including sending out free and paid press releases. You can use your Facebook, Twitter, LinkedIn, Instagram and other social media platforms to help build your following. Rather than repeat here the hundreds upon hundreds of suggestions on how to promote your blog, type "how to promote my blog" into your browser. You'll come up with more great ideas than I could mention here.

Finally, there may be no better resource for learning about blogging for artists than the Wet Canvas forums. Search for "wetcanvas.com internet sales strategies" and you'll find a couple sticky threads at the top of the page with hundreds of posts on blogging for artists, including some from me.

Additional Posts on Blogging from Art Marketing-News.com

How to Start an Art Blog
Blogging for Artists Trumps Social Media
Discover Why Blogging for Artists Pays Dividends
Five Ways Daily Blogging Provides Added Value to Your Art
52 Blog Topics for Artists
26 More Blog Topics for Artists

> (search for the exact titles on ArtMarketingNews.com
> to find and read these posts)

Blogging for some is intimidating at first. Give yourself a chance to find your voice. You have more to share and more to offer than you realize now. The amount of unique knowledge and intense passion you have on subjects close to your heart. Just as you share your art with the world, you can do the same with your blog.

CHAPTER 9

Social Media

When you give everyone a voice and give people power, the system usually ends up in a really good place. – Mark Zuckerberg

I could write a book on social media. Indeed, dozens of excellent ones have already been published. One of my favorites is *Crush It!: Why NOW Is the Time to Cash In on Your Passion*, a bestseller by Gary Vaynerchuk. In it he gives great examples of how to use social media, including suggestions on the best products and services to tap those resources.

As with blogging, the amount of available information on social media – from what it is to how to use it – is overwhelming, and it's all available with a few keyboard clicks. So I won't try to cover in this book this huge topic with a tremendous number of variables. You'll learn most of these things by trying them out and by doing your own research to discover what works best for you.

If I were going to recommend Twitter, I'd set aside any notions of giving you specific instructions here on how to use it effectively. Social media marketing possibilities can be overwhelming, so it can be overwhelming just to figure out where to begin, let alone spend your time in deciding which social media tool will give you the best bang for your effort and your buck. Nevertheless, I can help you in this quest because from experience I've developed strong preferences on your best options.

Concentrate on four social media and forget about the rest, or for the time being at least, give them only occasional explorations. My four top choices are the following. (Yours may differ.):

1. Facebook 2. Instagram 3. LinkedIn 4. YouTube

The size and significance of Facebook cannot be underestimated. I suggest you have an account in your name, preferably the same name as in your website domain. That's a matter of consistent branding. For instance, my Facebook address is www.facebook.com/barney.davey. Facebook's terms of service do not allow for business use in their personal accounts, but you can still set up a Facebook "Fan Page" or a "Group" for your business. Your Facebook personal account cannot have more than 5,000 friends.

The Difference Between a Facebook Fan Page and a Group

According to Mashable.com, Facebook Groups are set up for more personal interaction. Groups are also directly connected to the people who administer them, meaning that activities that go on there could reflect on you personally. Pages, on the other hand, don't list the names of administrators, and are thought of as a person, almost in the way that under the law a corporate entity is considered a "person."

Twitter and Tweet Management

A primary difference between Facebook and Twitter is the difference between closed versus open accessibility to the public. On Facebook I have to approve people who want to "friend" me so they can access my information. On Twitter, anyone can follow me, whether I decide to follow them back or not. For this reason, I feel Facebook is more homey or clubby than Twitter.

I recommend the same naming strategy for Twitter as I do on my website and my blog. Here again, my Twitter account name is www.twitter.com/barneydavey. In effect, I'm making my name my brand, but when that name branding isn't possible, I look for other ways to include my name. For instance, my blog title is Art Marketing News by Barney Davey. I want it to be easily understood that I am the author of the 300 posts written to help visual artists succeed at the business of art.

However, I do use Twitter to help expose my brand and expand my audience. I use software called Hoot Suite (www.hootsuite.com) to help manage my tweets. There are competitors such as Tweet Deck (www.tweetdeck.com) that do the same thing, which is to integrate social media platforms and allow you to publish on one and have the same information appear on the other automatically. A very nice feature of Hoot Suite is it allows you to create posts and set them up to post on day and time you choose.

YouTube and Vlogging

I've included YouTube among my top four platforms because video content is increasingly important. Google has a beta program called Gaudi that allows it to capture the spoken word to index and archive. So for those who think they should avoid vlogging (video blogging), think again. It can be a wonderful way to gain page rankings and stand out from your competitors who haven't caught on.

By using the internet and vlogging, Gary Vaynerchuk grew his father's discount liquor store from $4 million to $60 million in annual sales. In that process he has created more than 650 videos in which he answers questions about wine from viewers or discusses new or vintage wines from the store. His production technique is decidedly low-tech but highly effective nonetheless. So there's a message in that, too. All in all, his efforts have made him a bona fide internet marketing star, a sought-after speaker, and the subject of numerous traditional media interviews and stories.

Don't worry if you think that you won't come across as chic, hot or telegenic. Gary Vaynerchuk has proven that you don't need to be any of these to use video successfully. Besides, you have your art to talk about and display, which is and should be the real star anyway. I've blogged about Valentina at Val's Art Diary (www.valsartdiary.com) and Natasha Wescoat (wescoatfineart.com), and how both have used video to promote themselves and their art.

Of course, it's not lost on me that Val and Natasha are both what one of my readers called "adorable" in a comment to my post on them. While looks and personality may help drive some traffic, we're interested in real buyers – not wooing admirers. That means if you work on delivering solid content, you don't have to be on camera all the time. Find a way to let your personality and art shine through and you'll get results. Just like Gary Vaynerchuk.

There are other options to YouTube, including Dailymotion (www. Dailymotion), and Vimeo (www.vimeo.com). Done right, of course, any of these options can work for you. Still I'm comfortable with the millions of visitors and the name brand that YouTube offers.

When Twitter launched its popular Periscope – allowing users to do live broadcasting to their followers and anyone who clicks on a #hashtag related to the broadcast – it didn't take long for Facebook to come up with a rival product.

Facebook Live is fast becoming the preferred service for live streaming. The thing about live streaming is that it's not pretty. There are no pretenses. It's like having a conversation with someone you know whom you bumped into at the grocery store. It can be very effective for building a following and connecting with your "tribe." As for assistance in working with this site, there's a growing resource available that you can access by searching for "Facebook Live help."

Networking with LinkedIn

LinkedIn, number three on my list, is different from other social networks. It's more closed and attracts more professional types than either Facebook or Twitter. For instance, many *Fortune* 500 CEOs have profiles on that site.

Here's information about it directly from the site:
LinkedIn is an interconnected network of experienced professionals from around the world, representing 150 industries and 200 countries. You can find, be introduced to and collaborate with qualified professionals that you need to work with to accomplish your goals.

When you join, you create a profile that summarizes your professional expertise and accomplishments. You can use your connections to help develop professionally. Your network consists of your connections, your connections' connections and the people they know, linking you to a vast number of qualified professionals and experts.

What Your Network Allows You to Do:

- Manage the information that's publicly available about you as a professional.
- Find and be introduced to potential clients, service providers and recommended subject experts.
- Create and collaborate on projects, gather data, share files and solve problems.
- Be found for business opportunities and find potential partners.
- Gain new insights from discussions with likeminded professionals in private group settings.
- Discover inside connections that can help you land jobs and close deals.
- Post and distribute job listings to find the best talent for your company.

LinkedIn is set up and positioned as the professional's choice for social networking. There are some excellent groups you can join in which you can meet interesting and helpful people. You can use these groups to find answers to questions or get help for professional issues you might have.

Microsoft bought LinkedIn in 2016. It remains to be seen how that will affect the platform. My guess is it will be good for both companies.

What I find on LinkedIn are communities of artists seeking help and offering help. While there are some art appreciation groups represented, there are far more actual artists' groups on the site. I have nothing against participating in these groups and realize artists can find help and support in them. However, remember that your marketing goal should be to extend your reach to potential buyers, as opposed to making more contacts among fellow artists.

While my posts to social media go everywhere now, as is the case for many bloggers, you can find arguments that this social media strategy can't last. That's because the real-time effects of social media are already triggering the search engines themselves to find ways to include posts from social media. As a result, it's thought that having duplicate content might hinder your SEO for your tweets or Facebook posts, causing them to fall in search rankings. There are other reasons, but so far I'm not inclined to create unique content for different social media outlets. Who has the time? Give me enough motivation, however, and I'm sure I'll make the time if I have to.

Social media can flood your email, especially when you're building a following, but it is *so* worth it to control who you follow. The people (and the business pages) you're not interested in will fall away eventually when you don't follow back. I work at creating a community of followers on Facebook that are either family or friends, but mostly artists. I have the same mission on Twitter, but I include a mix of social media, business and tech gurus to help me stay informed on exciting developments in those fields.

My advice on all these social networks is to limit how much time you spend building relationships with other artists.

While you can use your connections with them in the networks to get help and answers, that's not the best business use of your time. Many of those questions posted in LinkedIn can be, or already have been, addressed on other discussion boards, such as on the copious threads on the General Business forum of WetCanvas.com.

As stated above, your mission in using social media is to make friends, associates and followers who are themselves potential buyers of your art or connections to people who are. You have limited time to work on your social networking. You're an artist, right? Yes, it can be instrumental in your career business growth, but only if you keep your focus on why you're concerned about that in the first place. Just remember, however enjoyable you might find social media sites, you're investing your valuable time on them for business and not for fun.

Though, as I said earlier, there's an overwhelming mother lode of information on using social media, I'd nevertheless direct you to one "nugget," a link to a series of articles published by Kate Harper on her blog. She's a greeting card designer who has published her own line of cards and now works with licensing companies. I've also provided an article for the series (http://kateharperblog.blog-spot.com/2010/03/social-media-month.html). You'll uncover a wealth of practical information and insights among the 22 contributors to the series.

If you dig into some of the many other resources– such as Flickr, Stumbleupon and more – I trust you'll mine them well and to your advantage. If, after you've examined what I've given here, you have the time and energy to dig for more, go for it. The ones I've provided are guaranteed to give you a solid ROI (return on your investment) of time and effort.

Is Article Marketing for You?

Article marketing is one last idea for you. It involves writing and publishing knowledgeable articles for online services such as for ehow.com and ezinearticles.com. Done well, article marketing can help establish your credibility and drive traffic to your blog or website. There are art-specific sites that take article submissions on a regular basis. A couple of notable examples are www.fineartstudiosonline.com and www.emptyeasel.com. Both publish frequently and are always seeking new voices to add to their mix. Here again, if you're not up the writing yourself, you can employ the services of a copywriter to ghostwrite articles on topics you choose.

Website Traffic to Your Website and Blog

I previously mentioned the purpose of social media is simple. Use it to generate awareness of you and your art. Additionally, you should seek to use it as a source of traffic to your blog and website. That's how I use social media. I do have some fun posting and interacting with friends and fans, particularly on Facebook. But I limit my time so it doesn't cut into more meaningful activities. And mostly I try to keep my posts art related, but not exclusively as I like variety and believe my followers do as well.

Another way to use social media is to do what I call "customer hunting." I find for most artists it's too expensive and time-consuming to advertise and frequently post with hopes of attracting their customer avatar. I've developed a much better way of honing in on your top prospects so that you can identify them by name, (yes, by name sometimes), groups and associations. I devote an entire lesson to how to go about doing this in my How to Find Collectors training. [bdavey.co/find]

By focusing on those people who are most like your avatar, you can get to the "know, like, trust" state faster. Plus, you can drastically cut down or eliminate your reliance on advertising to generate traffic to your online media properties. Besides showing you how to identify your best prospective buyers, I hope my shared experience, advice and knowledge have given you efficient ways to connect and stay in touch with them.

Resources

How to Find Art Buyers and Collectors

- How to Find Collectors training course – the most comprehensive course available for artists to discover the best ways to identify, connect with and sell their art to high-value collectors. [bdavey.co/find]

Website for Artists Services

- artistwebsite.org
- artsites.ca
- artspan.com
- artstorefronts.com
- artstudiosonline.com
- bigblackbag.com
- faso.com
- fineartamerica.com
- foliolink.com
- foliotwist.com
- heavybubble.com
- impactfolios.com
- otherpeoplespixels.com
- scotstyle.com
- sitewelder.com
- smugmug.com (created for photographers)
- xanadugallery.com

Free CDN and Performance Service

- Cloudflare.com – free, easy-to-use CDN service for any website

Generic Website Builders

- squarespace.com
- web.com
- wix.com
- weebly.com
- godaddy.com

Sites that Sell Art Prints:

- art.com
- allposters.com
- fineartmarketplace.com
- print-and-fulfill platforms
  - artistrising.com
  - artspan.com
  - cafepress.com
  - deviantart.com
  - fineartamerica.com
  - fineartmarketplace.com
  - imagekind.com
  - redbubble.com
  - zazzle.com

Fine art reproduction / giclee printing service

digitalartsstudio.net
fineartimpressions.com

Artist Community Websites

- ebsqart.com
- artflock. com

Artist Promotional Sites

Where you upload images to a gallery and fulfill upon sale

- artspan.com
- etsy.com
- yessy.com
- artbyus.com
- picassomio.com

Juried Sites

- saatchiart.com
- ugallery.com
- artfulhome.com
- artthatfits.com, and too many more to name

Physical Galleries with Online Galleries

XanaduGallery.com

250+ Places to Sell Your Art Online

ArtsyShark List of Online Art Sites - http://www.art-syshark.com/125-places-to-sell/

Search-Based Keyword and Analytics Tools

- Google Keyword Tool - google.com/adwords
- Google Analytics tool - google.com/analytics
- Google Search Console - google.com/webmasters/tools

Local Search Engines

- Google Local Business Center – www.google.com/lbc
- Yahoo Local – http://listings.local.yahoo.com/csubmit/index.php
- Microsoft (Bing) – https://ssl.bing.com/listings/ListingCenter.aspx

Free Privacy Statement Generator

- http://www.freeprivacypolicy.com

Whois Domain Ownership Lookup Tool

Ajax Whois - www.ajaxwhois.com

Graphic Design Tools

- pixlr.com
- canva.com
- canva design school
- picmonkey.com
- gimp.org

Email Service Providers

- Madmimi.com
- ActiveCampaign.com
- Aweber.com
- MailChimp.com

Marketing Automation Services (Including Email)

- Infusionsoft.com
- ActiveCampaign.com
- GetDrip.com
- Convertkit.com
- Rainmakerplatform.com

You'll find MailChimp and Aweber also offer marketing automation options. They're harder to use and not as robust as others on this list. Rainmaker is a complete solution. I tried it and it didn't meet my needs. It has thousands of other users, so it might have been my needs not fulfilled.

I use Infusionsoft now. It's expensive and not recommended for you unless your list is greater than 5,000 subscribers. I recommend starting with ActiveCampaign as you can grow with it. Convertkit is used by many top bloggers, including Pat Flynn. GetDrip was purchased by LeadPages in 2016. It's a solid platform. As with all your choices, do your due diligence and research to make the best decision for your business.

ABOUT THE AUTHOR

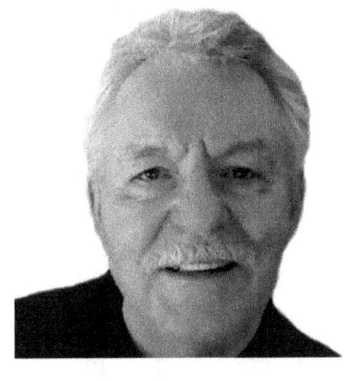

My name is Barney Davey and I'm the proud author of this book.

I help artists and photographers to find new buyers, sell more art and market their work efficiently.

If you're an artist or photographer, or work as an entrepreneur in a creative field, I'm here to help you create a successful, sustainable and rewarding career. You'll find numerous ways to grow your career through my books, blog posts, workshops, online training, consulting and more.

I began advising artists when I joined *Decor* magazine and the *Decor* Expo trade shows as a marketing executive in 1988. Both were influential, prominent art business leaders.

Decor was in the business of helping artists, galleries and picture framers for more than 135 years. At its peak, the *Decor* Expo Atlanta Show was ranked in the top 100 among more than 10,000 annual trade shows produced in the U.S.

During my career, I attended around 200 art trade shows where I got to know top artists and successful publishers. I used this unique opportunity to study their best marketing practices. Those events, plus my sales, marketing and entrepreneurial experiences, form the crucible of the experience, knowledge and wisdom I share with artists today.

Each of my five books on art marketing has been a "Business of Art" bestseller on Amazon.com

You can get a clear idea of the marketing insights and industry knowledge I share by visiting Art Marketing News. You'll find more than 600 art business and marketing posts. Art Marketing News is ranked # 1 by Art Business News.

A Path to a Rewarding Career

My work with artists, photographers and fine art print publishers on their plans to grow their businesses gave me experiences that lit a path to my future. With the collective knowledge, wisdom and inspiration I gained, I've built a business based on purpose, passion and prosperity.

Other Bestselling Art Marketing Books by Barney Davey

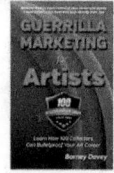 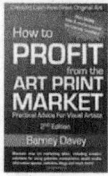 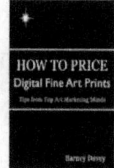 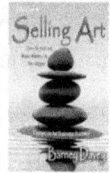 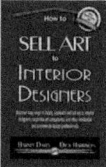

All are available on Amazon.com http://bdavey.co/books

How to Find Collectors Training Course

To sell art, you need buyers. You can only sell to two types of people:

1) Strangers

2) People who know you.

That's it. You know it's much easier to sell to people who know you. Selling to strangers is expensive, exhausting and stressful. It's mostly a frustrating waste of time.

What artists learn in this course is how to identify their top prospects – often by – how to connect with them and stay in touch with them.

Build the relationships first and sales and referrals will follow. It is a natural progression with a snowballing effect. It only requires you to stay proactive in following the training.

This Training Is My Masterpiece.

Artists using who tap into the training benefit from my 30 years of helping artists market their work. I am pumped about its career changing potential and as such am eager to share it with as many artists as possible.

I want you to enjoy the success you know you can have. I don't know of a better way to build a successful long-term career than to develop personal relationships with people who love your work and admire you for making it.

Go to http://bdavey.co/find for all the details.